Krishna Deities and Their Miracles

How the Images of Lord Krishna Interact With Their Devotees

By
Stephen Knapp

Dedicated to
all those who are trying to attain
higher levels of spiritual experience.
This is to show that raising our love of God
brings God closer to us,
and He can reveal Himself to whoever He wants
in whatever way He wants.

Published through the efforts of
The World Relief Network
Detroit, Michigan

Cover Print: A beautifully decorated Deity of Lord Sri Krishna.

ISBN 13: 978-1463734299
ISBN 10: 1463734298

Other books by the author:

1. The Secret Teachings of the Vedas: The Eastern Answers to the Mysteries of Life
2. The Universal Path to Enlightenment
3. The Vedic Prophecies: A New Look into the Future
4. How the Universe was Created and Our Purpose In It
5. Toward World Peace: Seeing the Unity Between Us All
6. Facing Death: Welcoming the Afterlife
7. The Key to Real Happiness
8. Proof of Vedic Culture's Global Existence
9. The Heart of Hinduism: The Eastern Path to Freedom, Enlightenment and Illumination
10. The Power of the Dharma: An Introduction to Hinduism and Vedic Culture
11. Vedic Culture: The Difference it can Make in Your Life
12. Reincarnation & Karma: How They Really Affect Us
13. The Eleventh Commandment: The Next Step for Social Spiritual Development
14. Seeing Spiritual India: A Guide to Temples, Holy Sites, Festivals and Traditions
15. Crimes Against India: And the Need to Protect its Ancient Vedic Tradition
16. Destined for Infinity, a spiritual adventure in the Himalayas
17. Yoga and Meditation: Their Real Purpose and How to Get Started
18. Avatars, Gods and Goddesses of Vedic Culture: Understanding the Characteristics, Powers and Positions of the Hindu Divinities
19. The Soul: Understanding Our Real Identity
20. Prayers, Mantras and Gayatris: A Collection for Insights, Protection, Spiritual Growth, and Many Other Blessings

You can find out more about Stephen Knapp
and his books, free Ebooks, research,
and numerous articles and photos,
along with many other spiritual resources at:
http://www.Stephen-Knapp.com

Contents

INTRODUCTION

The reason why we are using the word "miracles" in the title is because many people are familiar with this word and its connotation to that which is out of the ordinary or of a special nature in the area of spiritual or religious topics. And many of the pastimes that we relate in this book can be considered in that way. Herein we will read some of the pastimes about how the temple Deities act in personal ways in the lives of Their devotees, both in waking life as well as in dreams that affect the existence of such devotees. This is with one's personal Deities as well. But for the Indian Vedic community, especially those who follow the deeper aspects of Santana-dharma, many of these descriptions are not so much miracles, but are considered common events that many people experience as part of their devotion to the Deities in the temple.

It is understood in the Vedic tradition that a person who raises his or her consciousness through spiritual practice can attain the perception of various levels of the spiritual realm, as well as perceive the higher dimensions of existence. But this depends on how sincere and steady they are in their spiritual practice. However, for one who has not endeavored in this way, all of this may seem like a mirage, a misconception, or simple buffoonery. They may be convinced that such things cannot happen, or that the Deity is not real, only a statue. But such people only reveal themselves to be both without knowledge of God or a perception of the higher dimension, and certainly without any spiritual experience. Thus, if people like this advocate a view that such things are not possible while being without knowledge or perception, or remain closed to the potential that such things can happen, then they remain but fools, closed to the evidence, the scriptural instructions, and the stories of personal experiences from those who have had them.

However, even those who blindly accept that God can interact with us without having perceived it, must also go deeper than that. They must also participate in the genuine spiritual path that uplifts or spiritualizes their consciousness so they can also begin to perceive that which is spiritual. That is what makes the difference and opens them up to the possibilities and probabilities of them having their own spiritual experiences in any number of ways, including the likes of those described herein.

These descriptions of miracles, or the interactions between the Deities of Krishna and the devotees, will cover a wide range of occurrences. Some of these miracles may be considered minor or more ordinary, while others may be a special spiritual phenomena that shows the definite interplay of the Supreme Being with His devotees and the spiritual dimension overlapping into the material realm.

These descriptions of Krishna Deities and His various forms and other Divinities include traditional pastimes that have been recorded from years ago, as well as those that are more recent. It shows how great or even minor devotees can have experiences with Krishna as long as they have two qualities, which is great faith and love. A variety of situations are provided in these descriptions, which shows the many ways that the Lord can reveal Himself, and the favor that is shown by Him to those who worship Him.

Why should some of these descriptions of the activities of these Deities be considered special, which involve what are often viewed as mere images in the temples? Because it shows how the Supreme Being and His expansions can reveal Him or Herself in many ways to the amusement and to the awe of the devotees, based on the devotees' love and devotion. Some of these revelations are like the play or pastimes of the Supreme Lord, while others are for heightening the realizations or guidance of the devotees, and those who hear about such pastimes. It is to our benefit to consider the information that is provided, and to listen or read these stories to get a better understanding of the potential relations that take place between the Supreme and His devotees. It also gives an indication of the possibility of what can happen to any of us. You will notice that the basis of all these experiences that are related in the stories that follow is but one thing, and that is love. The more there is love for the Lord by the devotee, the more compelled the Lord is to reveal Himself or interact in the lives of those devotees. Why? This will be explained later in the book.

CHAPTER ONE

The Antiquity of Deity Worship in The Vedic Tradition

There have been some people who have declared that the worship of Deities or images or the *murti* in the temples is but a recent invention of Vedic culture. However, that is not an accurate point. It is true that according to the different *yugas* or ages (such as Satya-yuga, Treta-yuga, Dvapara-yuga, and Kali-yuga) there are different processes for spiritual development that have been more recommended than others. For example, meditation was the recommended process for Satya-yuga, when people lived much longer and could sit in concentration or in *samadhi* for long periods of time. Then in Treta-yuga it was best to engage in various and extravagant rituals, *havans*, *yajnas*, or fire ceremonies. Then in Dvapara-yuga it was best to engage in elaborate worship, with opulent offerings to the Deities and prayers and mantras sung to the Deities. So, all of these processes have continued down through the ages to some degree or another. However, in Kali-yuga, though we still see all of these processes used, it is now the chanting of mantras, especially the Hare Krishna mantra, that is the most highly efficient and recommended process of spiritual growth in this age.

So, Deity worship as seen in the temples has been around for thousands of years. And as evidence of that, we can find references in the Vedic texts, as well as in the historical holy sites around India.

HISTORICAL SITES OF ANCIENT DEITY WORSHIP

For example, seven kilometers south of Gokula, not far from Mathura, is the Dauji temple. Dauji is the Deity of Lord Balarama that was originally installed 5,000 years ago by King Vajranabha, Krishna's great-grandson. From Lord Krishna and His queen Rukmini was born the great warrior Pradyumna, one of His prominent sons, who married the daughter of Rukmi, Rukmavati. They gave birth to Anirudha. Anirudha married Rukmi's son's daughter, Rachana, and from her was born Vajra, who would remain among the few survivors of the Yadus' battle. (*Bhagavatam* 10.90.35-37)

In fact, King Vajra established a number of Krishna Deities in the area. The present Dauji temple that we see today was built 200 years ago by Shyama Das of Delhi. Many people also attend this temple to get *darshan* of the single Deity of the 6 feet tall Lord Balarama. From the other side of the temple you can see the Deity of Revati, Lord Balarama's wife. Nearby is the Balabhadra Kund or Kshira (milk) Sagara (sea) where the Deity of Lord Balarama had been hidden during the Moghul invasion. Near this kund is a temple to Harideva, and in the bazaar is another temple to Krishna as Banke Bihari.

There is also much history on the site of Krishna's birth, the Krishna Janmasthana in Mathura. Historical records indicate that the first temple here was also built by King Vajranabha. This temple lasted for many years. The next temple was supposedly built by King Vikramaditya in 400 BCE. That was destroyed by the infamous Mahmud Ghazni in 1017-18. Ancient descriptions relate that such a magnificent building would have taken 200 years of great toil by the world's greatest craftsmen. Thereafter, a third temple was built by a citizen named Jajja during the time of King Vijayapalavadeva, ruler of Mathura, according to an inscription on a stone slab discovered in the area. Sri Chaitanya visited this temple during His visit in 1515. Unfortunately, that was destroyed by the Muslim Sikander Lodi shortly thereafter. The next temple was built by Raja Virsinghadeva Bundela during the reign of Jehangir (around 1650). It is said that this temple stood 250 feet tall and was a stately structure made of intricately carved red sandstone, costing some 33 lakhs of rupees. But again it was destroyed by the fanatic Muslim Aurangzeb in 1669-70. Then it its place a mosque was built, which still stands today. The next temple over the place of Krishna's birth appeared later in the mid-20th century.

Also in Mathura, not far from the Dwarkadish Mandira, there is the temple of white Sweta-Varaha, and another of Adi-Varaha. According to local history as explained by local pandits, back in Satya-yuga this Deity had been given to Lord Indra who worshiped Him in Swarga, his heavenly abode. The Deity was later taken by Ravana when he defeated Indra who took Him to Sri Lanka. Then, after Ravana was defeated by Lord Ramachandra, the Deity was taken to Ayodhya by Lord Ramachandra. Lord Ramachandra gave it to His brother Satrughna who brought it to Mathura when he was dispatched to conquer Madhu Daitya and Lavanasura. After defeating the demonic father and son, Madhu and Lavanasura, he installed the Deity of Adi-Varaha here. This story is more fully explained in Chapter 163 of the *Varaha Purana*.

East of Mathura is Vrindavana, and in Vrindavan is the Radha-Govindaji temple that is another of the seven major temples of Vrindavan. It is across the road and a little farther down the street from the Rangaji temple. It was established by Rupa Gosvami where he discovered the Gopala Deity. The beautiful temple is made out of red sandstone and was completed in 1590. The temple is now only two storeys tall but once reached up to seven storeys. The Muslim fanatic Aurangzeb, doing his dirty work, dismantled the upper five storeys of the temple due to his envy. While his men were destroying the temple, there was a loud thunderous noise that shook the ground. This put fear into the hearts of the men and they immediately stopped and ran away. Due to fear of the Moghuls, before they arrived the devotees moved the original Deities to Jaipur where today many pilgrims go to see them. So the temple now has *pratibhuh* Deities, or representative expansions, of the original Radha-Govindaji that are worshiped. The original Govindaji Deity is said to have been installed in Vrindavan thousands of years ago by Vajranabha.

Also, in Vrindavan, farther into the eastern part of town, are many other temples, including the large and ornate Lala Babu Mandir with Deities of Radha, Krishna, and Lalita. Then at the corner where we turn off from Loi Bazaar to go toward the Banke Bihari Mandir, we find the Gopishwara Mahadeva Shiva temple with a Shiva *linga*, said to have been originally installed by Krishna's great-grandson, Vajranabha, and is the place where Lord Shiva did austerities in hopes of entering the *rasa-lila* dance as a *gopi* (cow-herd girl). In the morning devotees wash the *linga* with milk and other items, and then later the *pujaris* dress the *linga* in bright colored clothes.

A few miles from Barsana is Nandagram, another place where Krishna performed many childhood pastimes described in the *Bhagavatam*. On top of the hill is the main temple that has Deities of Krishna, Balarama, Nanda Maharaja (Krishna's father), Mother Yashoda, Srimati Radharani, and two of Krishna's friends. There is also a Shiva *lingam* in a small shrine across from the temple called Nandisvara, which again is said to have been installed by Vajranabha many hundreds of years ago. It is considered that this hill is an incarnation of Lord Shiva. From the top of the walls that surround the temple we can get good views of the area, and someone who is familiar with it can point out other nearby places connected with Krishna's pastimes that we may want to visit.

Now, let us go into the foothills of the large Girnar Hill in Gujarat where we find the Radha-Damodara temple with beautiful Deities of Krishna's four-armed form. As Lakshmi-Narayana, the Deities are formed of the typical black and brown stone, and are described in the *Skanda Purana* as being self-manifested over 12,000 years ago. Next to the main temple is another for Lord Balarama and Revati, His consort. The original temple at this site is said to have been built 4500 years ago by Vajranath, Lord Krishna's grandson. Not far away is a place where lived Vallabha, the 16th century Vaishnava *acharya*.

Another interesting story is in regard to Guruvayoor in Kerala, South India, which has the Deity of a four-armed standing Vishnu with a *chakra* in the right hand, conchshell in the left, and mace and lotus flower in the other two. Sri Krishna showed this form of His only twice during His appearance on earth: once to Arjuna just before the battle of Kurukshetra while speaking the *Bhagavad-gita*, and once to His parents, Vasudeva and Devaki, at the time of His birth. This Deity is said to have been worshiped by Lord Krishna Himself at

Dwaraka thousands of years ago. The legend is that when Krishna left this world, He gave the Deity to His devotee Uddhava to look after it. He then ordered Brihaspati, the guru or spiritual teacher of the demigods, and Vayu, demigod of the wind, to take care of this Vishnu Deity and to install it somewhere for the benefit of humanity. When they arrived at Dwaraka to get the Deity, the city of Dwaraka had already sunk into the sea. After searching in the water, they found the Deity and went south. Not knowing where to go, they sat down by the side of a lake and began to meditate. Soon, Shiva appeared and after some discussion they decided to start a new temple for the Deity of Vishnu near the Rudratirtha Lake. Since that time 5,000 years ago, the place has been known as Guruvayoor (guru for Brihaspati and vayoor for Vayu). Hundreds of devotees visit the temple everyday for seeing the Deity. Western devotees, however, are not allowed in without a letter of permission from the Arya Samaj.

Going eastward we go to Simhachalam. There we find the Jiyada Narasimha temple. It is here where Lord Narasimha's devotee Prahlada is said to have built the original shrine when he was saved from his father Hiranyakashipu. The story is that the hill at Simhachalam is the one from which the demon Hiranyakashipu had his devotee son thrown from it in an attempt to kill him. The mountain was also placed over Prahlada, but the Lord saved him by jumping over the hill and lifting Prahlada from the sea. The hill may seem somewhat lopsided since it is also accepted that the Lord had lifted the hill enough for Prahlada to escape from underneath it. Thereafter, Prahlada asked the Lord to assume a Deity form as both Lord Narasimha (the lion form) who would soon kill Hiranyakashipu, and Lord Varaha (the boar *avatara*) who had already killed Hiranyakshya, the brother of Hiranyakashipu. Thus, the Deity is of Varaha Narasimha.

When Hiranyakashipu was later killed by Lord Narasimha, Prahlada built a temple around the Deity where worship was conducted. In time, however, the temple was neglected and earth covered the Deity. Much later, the king of the lunar dynasty, Pururava, was drawn to Simhachalam and rediscovered the Deity under the earth. Hearing a voice, it instructed him to cover the Deity with sandalwood paste and worship Him, and only uncover Him once a year. This practice has continued and they have an annual festival when everyone can see the Deity without it being covered in sandalwood. Pururava also rebuilt the temple and established the worship of the Deity again, which has continued to this day.

Also, we can take note of the famous Kanaka Durga temple on the hilltop that overlooks the town of Vijayawada. This Deity is considered to be self-manifested. It is said that Adi Shankara had worshiped the goddess here, as well as Agastya Muni, Markandeya, and even the Pandavas, all of which suggests how old this Deity is. Legend relates that she killed the powerful demon Durgama in this area, and is presently accepted as the protector of the city. This is an interesting temple and many people come to see it. You can see families arrive to see the Deities and to perform their *puja* together.

At the nearby Mangalagiri hills, the Pana-Narasimha temple is at the top of a flight of 600 steps on the hillside. The Deity called Pana Narasimha is worshiped only with offerings of water mixed with jaggery, which is a mixture of raw cane sugar, camphor, cardamom, and black pepper. He drinks only half of the offerings while the other half goes for the devotees. It is said that in times long ago other ingredients used to be offered. This is explained in a story. The sage Kashyapa Prajapati had one son, Namuchi, who was a cruel demon. To acquire powers, Namuchi underwent severe austerities which produced intense flames from his body. The fire became so powerful that it began to flow through the universe. The demigods could not withstand the heat that was spreading, so they went to Brahma about this matter. Brahma went to Namuchi to appease him by granting him a boon. Namuchi asked to never be killed by anything either wet or dry, which Brahma granted. After that he was overconfident and began harassing the demigods, who then had to go to Lord Vishnu. He assured them that Namuchi's end would come at the right time.

Later, during a battle which involved Indra killing the armies of Namuchi, Lord Vishnu in His form as Lord Narasimha took His disk and dipped it into some foam, which was neither wet nor dry, and then gave it to Indra who threw it at Namuchi. Namuchi fled and even went into a cave at Mangalagiri, hiding by giving up his physical form. But the disk followed and killed him there. The blood that began to flow turned into a stream called Raktakalya that spread into the area. Red soil surrounds the temple to this day. The Devas were fearful of the Lord as Narasimha, so they offered Him divine nectar to drink. He drank only half of it and said that in Satya-yuga he would drink only half of the nectar offered to Him. In Treta-yuga He would drink ghee. In Dvapara-yuga He would drink milk from a Kamadhenu cow, and in Kali-yuga He would drink half of the sweet jaggery water that was offered to Him. This is why He only accepts half of the offering, leaving the rest as *prasada* to be accepted by the devotees.

The next place we can go is 200 kilometers south from Hyderbad to Srisailam. This town is next to the Krishna River. It is found on Rishabhagiri Hill. It is mentioned in the *Mahabharata* and the *Puranas*, which indicates its antiquity. It has the Mallikarjuna (Shiva) temple, known as one of the 12 *jyotirlinga* (self-manifesting *linga*) temples in India. It is a large temple, built in 1404-5 by King Harihara Raya. There is a hall of finely carved stone work, beautiful silver doors, and a huge Nandi. The original Shiva *linga* is to the right of the main temple. This temple was visited by Adi Shankara and later by Lord Chaitanya, as well as by Lord Narasimha's devotee Prahlada and Lord Rama, who is said to have installed the Sahasra *linga*, noticeable by the three-headed Naga which surrounds it. Therefore, it is an extremely ancient site. There are also the Panchapandavas, the five *lingas* installed by the five Pandava brothers found in the courtyard. The Parvati (Bhramarambika) temple, one of the 54 *Shakti-peeths*, is up a flight of stairs behind the Shiva temple. Parvati took the form of a bee to kill the Mahisasura demon, the buzzing of which you can still hear by putting your ear to a small hole in the back wall of the sanctum. Other shrines around the temple are for Chandramamba, Rajarajeshwari, Virabhadra, and Annapoorni.

Tirupati, in the Tirumalla Hills, has one of the most famous of the ancient temples. The legend behind the temple to the Deity of Lord Balaji is summarized as follows: Once Bhrigu insulted Mahavishnu, which annoyed Goddess Lakshmi. She then went to earth and did penance in Kolhapur, a location of another famous temple for Lakshmi. The Lord then came in search for the Goddess and arrived at these hills and stayed as Srinivasa. Here He met Padmavathi, an incarnation of Bhudevi and a princess of

Narayanapuram, whom He had promised to marry when He appeared as Lord Rama. When He married Her, it was a huge wedding, and the pastime was that He needed extra funds. He borrowed it from Kubera, the treasurer of the demigods. Kubera insisted on repayment with interest. Hence, the devotees in Andhra Pradesh call the Deity Vaddi Kasulaswamy (the Lord of interest), repaying Kubera's interest which never ends. The demigod Kubera is enshrined in the Govindaraja Swamy temple, believed to be there collecting the interest with a brass measure. Thus, somehow, many funds are always coming into the temple. In this way, this temple at Tirupati represents a tradition that goes back many, many hundreds of years.

Thirukkovilur is our next stop of temples with Deities that go back many years. It is located about 35 kilometers south of Tiruvannamali and 40 km west of Villupuram. Its history makes it occupy a distinct place in Vaishnava history. It is one of the 108 Divya Desams of Lord Vishnu. The Kshetra Khanda section in the *Padma Purana* discusses some of the glories of this holy place. It is associated with the Trivikrama *avatara* of Lord Vishnu. After Trivikrama or Lord Vamana had taken the whole universe with three steps from Bali Maharaja, ablution to Trivikrama's feet was performed by Brahma with the sacred waters of the Ganges. That water trickled off His feet and took the form of the sacred tank called the Chakra Tirtha. Indra is said to have had a dip in that water tank, and regained his lost possessions that had been taken by Bali.

Vaithisvarankoil is a small village about 25 to 30 miles south from Chidambaram, and just south of Sirkazhi. The stone temple has long halls with numerous columns. At the sanctum, I easily entered and the guard there was kind enough to show me around and explain a few things. I was able to get *darshan* of the main temple sanctum of Sri Vaidyanathaswamy, as well as the other smaller shrines for the other divinities. The shrine for Murugan is said to be where he received his trident. And the Jatayu Kundam or pond found off the southern hallway is where Jatayu, the great devotee bird of Lord Rama, had his last rites performed by Lord Rama.

Tirucherai is a small village located 15 kilometers southeast from Kumbakonam on the main road to Tiruvarur. Tirucherai, which like many villages may not be on the map, is one of the 108 Divya

Desams of Lord Vishnu. It is here at the Saranatha Perumal temple where the Deity of MahaVishnu resides.

The temple compound occupies 1½ acres of land (116 meters in length, 72 meters wide). In front of the temple is the large Sara Pushkarini water tank, which also occupies the same dimensions. The front gate of the temple complex has a fine looking nine-tiered *gopuram* that rises 120 feet tall. Inside the front gate is an additional but smaller *gopuram* of two tiers that leads into the temple. The sanctum is guarded by two sculpted *dwarapalas* or guards. Inside the sanctum, Saranatha Perumal, the presiding MahaVishnu Deity appears in a standing pose that is twelve feet tall while facing east. He is carved from black stone but is adorned with silver hands and chest plate. It is very auspicious to have *darshan* of this Deity. On the left side is the personification of the Cauvery River, and on the right is the sage Markandeya. In front is the smaller *utsavar* festival Deity of Saranatha, accompanied by Bhudevi, Sridevi, and Neeladevi. Actually, the presence of all five consorts of Vishnu, namely Sridevi, Neeladevi, Bhudevi, Saranayaki Amman, and Mahalakshmi within the same temple is a unique feature that is not found in other Vaishnava temples.

Many other shrines also exist within the temple, so there are numerous blessings we can receive by visiting each of them. First, another Deity of Vishnu as Sri Rajagopalaswamy occupies a separate shrine, and is accompanied by His consorts Rukmini and Satyabhama. Another shrine has Lord Venkatesha as Thiruvenkatamudayan. The metal Deities of Sri Rama, Sita, and Lakshmana are in another shrine, as well as Lakshmi-Narasimha. Other shrines are for Kaliyamardhana, Balasaranatha, Senai Mudaliar, Manavala Munigal, Ramanuja, and the twelve Alwars. At the southwestern corner of the Sara Pushkarini lake is a separate shrine for Cauvery who is seen embracing the child form of Vishnu. Images of Brahma and MahaVishnu are also there. This represents the austerity Cauvery Devi performed in order to gain the favor of the Lord.

Texts such as the *Brahmanda Purana*, the *Bhavishya Purana* (Chapters 68-72), and the *Maheswara Narada Samvardha* offer descriptions of the importance of this *tirtha* and pastimes related to it. One of the pastimes is described how Lord Shiva explained the significance of Tirucherai to the sage Narada Muni. The story is that on the eve of the universal deluge MahaVishnu ordered Brahma to safely keep the sacred Vedic texts, like the *Vedas, Agamas, Sashtras,* and *Puranas* in an enormous earthen pot. But with every attempt the pot would brake. He felt discouraged and prayed to MahaVishnu about this. Vishnu then told him that there are twelve Vaishnava holy places that are the most sacred. These included Sri Rangam, Tirupati, Kanchipuram, Tirunarayanapuram, SriMushnam, Naimisaranya, Kumbakonam, Vrishabathri, Ayodhya, Badarikashrama, and Sara Kshetram (Tirucherai). Out of all of these, He regarded Sara Kshetra as the most sacred. The hallowed center is graced with nine sacred *tirthas* of which the Sara Pushkarini Lake is the highest. So he instructed Brahma to journey to this place and take a dip in the Sara Pushkarini Lake and form a pot from the clay found in the lake. This would be successful. This is the lake located across the street in front of the temple.

So Brahma went there and he felt greatly satisfied. He then had a dip into the sacred lake and formed a pot from its clay. The earthen pot stood firm, much to his surprise. Brahma then stored all the major Vedic texts within it and kept them safe. Thus, his mission was complete. It is also believed that the seven great *rishis*, namely Bhrigu, Sowraga, Vyasa, Markandeya, Parasara, Vamadeva, and Baninthrathiya, continue to perform penances here to preserve the holy sanctity of the place. Thus, the antiquity of this temple and its holy shrines go back many hundreds of years.

The Senneriappa Iswara temple, a noted Shiva temple, can also be found in this town along the southern bank of the Cauvery River. This is not far from the Vishnu temple described above. It is smaller but no less sacred, and the priests are glad to see visitors. In front of the temple is a lake that is said to have been formed by a drop of ambrosia. It is called Jnanavavi or Bindhusuda. It has a small three-tiered *gopuram* over the second entrance into the temple. Passing through a few hallways one can reach the place of the presiding Deity. This is the Shiva *linga* known as Senneriappar or Sara Parameswara. It was the sage Markandeya who, so many years ago, installed a *linga* in this temple, which is now in the inner sanctum. The sage worshipped it everyday. Surya the Sun-god also is said to have atoned for his participation in Daksha's ritual here. Every year the rays of the sun grace the presiding *linga* for three days in the month of Masi (Feb-Mar). In the inner hallway are other shrines for various Shaivite saints. There are also three images of Durga and two of Chandeswara that are also in this temple. The outer walls of the main shrine have lovely sculptures that depict the pastimes of this place.

If you have stayed at Thiruvarur, then it is easy to take a morning bus for a short day trip east to Nagappattinam. It is on the seashore 24 km east of Thiruvarur, or 70 km east of Tanjore. This town has a Vishnu temple with three full sized Vishnu Deities that are standing, sitting, and lying on Ananta Sesha. It is a Divya Desam, one of the 108 most important Vishnu temples in India. You go in the front entrance, down a hallway and into the main temple hall and then into the sanctum. This is surrounded by a courtyard wherein we find a few other shrines, such as to Lakshmi. Once inside the sanctum you can see the smaller brass standing Vishnu Deity with Sridevi and Bhudevi at His sides. Behind Them is the main Deity, Sundaryarajan, who stands over 15 feet tall. He is spectacular, made of shiny black stone, but He and His ornaments and weapons are covered with solid silver, with a gold Lakshmi on His chest. He is really something to see and I was in awe gazing at Him. This was the whole reason for coming here, and I was glad to do so. After the crowd moved on, I was able to get a close up view. Afterwards I was able to circumambulate the temple and view the other shrines.

The *Brahmananda Purana* explains that this temple, called the Soundarvaraja Perumal temple, has existed in all four *yugas*, beginning with Satya-yuga. The legend is that Nagapattinam was originally called Soundaranyam. The name Nagapattinam, which means City of the Serpent, is derived from the fact that Adisesha, in Satya-yuga, performed austerities here to get the blessing to be able to stay forever in the presence of his Lord, Vishnu. The *Purana* also relates how Dhruva also performed austerities in this place. Dhruva's intention was to get the Lord to appear before him and then ask for the blessing of becoming ruler of the entire world. However, when Dhruva saw Lord Vishnu, he was so overwhelmed by the Lord's beauty that he was entirely content and forgot his materialistic wish.

He then simply requested the Lord to remain in Nagapattinam as Soundarya Rajan, "The King of Beauty," and bless the devotees. This is how the temple was manifested.

Another important and ancient temple is in Tiruchirappali, otherwise called Trichy or Sri Rangam. It is said the town was originally known as Tirusirappally, named after the three-headed *asura* Tirusiras who got a blessing from Lord Shiva after worshiping him here. Trichy has three major attractions. One is the Rock Fort temple in the heart of the old city. To get there we board the bus near our hotel and ride to a place several blocks away from the hilltop temple. We walk past the Teppakulam water tank and find the entrance to the Rock Fort temple in the Chinna Bazaar. We leave our shoes at the shoe minder's stall and proceed up more than 400 steps that are cut through the rock of the hill. It is a steep and laborious climb to the summit 273 feet up where the views are great. If it is not too hazy, you can see the Sri Rangam temple to the north. Westerners are, unfortunately, not allowed inside the hilltop temple to see the image of Vinayaka, known here as Uchi Pillayar.

Nonetheless, the Puranic legend of this Deity, as explained in the *Sri Ranga Mahatmya*, is that after Lord Brahma had done penance to help in the creation of the universe, when Brahma was in a state of deep meditation, Lord Vishnu was pleased with him. So Lord Vishnu manifested Himself as the Deity of Lord Ranganatha, known as Ranga Vimana, a form of Vishnu reclining on Seshanaga, the Lord's great serpent servant. Brahma worshiped Lord Ranganatha for many years and later gave the Deity to Vivasvan, the sun-god, who later handed the Deity over to Svayambhuva Manu. Manu passed on the Deity to King Ikshvaku, the great leader of the solar dynasty in which Lord Krishna would later appear as Lord Ramachandra.

Lord Ramachandra gave the Deity to Vibhishana, who was a great devotee and brother of the demon Ravana of the *Ramayana* epic. Vibhishan was returning to Sri Lanka from Ayodhya with the Vishnu Deity that had been presented to him by Lord Rama. However, he had been told that if he should set the Deity down on the ground, he would not be able to move it again. However, the gods were not pleased that the Deity would be taken away from the area of India and devised a plan to keep the deity in Bharat. Thus, when

Vibhashan stopped at Sri Rangam to take bath and perform his worship on the banks of the Kaveri River at a holy place called Chandra Pushkarini, he gave the Deity to a brahmana boy with instructions not to place it on the ground. But the boy, who was Lord Ganesh in disguise, placed it on the earth anyway. Then the Deity became firmly fixed to the ground and could not be moved from the spot where it remains to this day. Vibhishan became angry and chased the boy who ran to the summit of the hill that is the Rock Fort today. There Vibhishan caught and struck the boy, who then revealed his real form and stood transformed as Vinayaka. Even though Vibhishan begged to apologize before going on to Sri Lanka, the image of Vinayaka still has a depression on his face where he had been struck.

Another part of the tradition is that a king, Dharma Varma, had seen Lord Ranganatha in Ayodhya, Lord Ramachandra's capital, and prayed to worship Him. So the Lord blessed the king to stay at Sri Rangam. Nonetheless, the Deity also blessed Vibhishana by promising to always look toward his kingdom. This is why the Deity reclines with His head to the west, looking toward the south in the direction of Sri Lanka, Vibhishana's kingdom.

King Dharma Varma and his dynasty of the Chola kings built a large temple around Lord Ranganatha. The worship was quite opulent. But, unfortunately, things declined and gradually the temple was forgotten and covered over by a thick forest. The Deity was only discovered thousands of years later by a Chola king who accidently found it while chasing a parrot. The parrot explained that Lord Ranganatha was buried in the sand. So the king excavated the temple and restored it. It was the king who again established the Sri Rangam temple. Over time, many other Chola kings again expanded the temple, which is presently one of the largest temples in India.

However, the 14th century saw the invading Moghuls plunder most of the Lord's treasures from this temple. The Vijayanagar and Nayak rulers again revived it in the 15th and 16th centuries. Then in the 17th and 18th centuries, the Muslims, French, and then the British used the fortress in furthering their domination over the area. Only after India gained independence in 1947 did the Indian government and the Ramanujas or Sri Vaishnavas finally gain control to oversee the temple properly.

Another ancient temple is found at Tiruthangal (Tiruttangal), a town located two kilometers north of Sivakasi, which is about 18 km east from Srivilliputtur. It is reached by bus from places like Madurai, Srivilliputhur, Sankarankoil, and Virudhunagar. It has the Ninra Narayana Perumal temple.

The temple faces south on a small 100-foot tall hill in the northern part of town. Climbing the stairs, one reaches the spacious entranceway. A sculpture of Narayana Ramanuja, who was the person who spent much of his money to build this hallway, adorns one of the pillars. In the back and to the west is the cave temple wherein we find the Deity of Pallikonda Perumal, Lord Vishnu in His reclining pose. Sridevi and Bhudevi are at His feet while sages like Markandeya and Bhrigu are on either side. The history of this place is that once Lord Ranganatha journeyed to Srivilliputhur to seek Sri Andal for marriage and spent the night here.

The history of this place goes back to a time when the three main Devis, namely Sridevi, Bhudevi, and Neeladevi, wondered who was most favored by Lord Vishnu. Sridevi (Lakshmi) wanted to prove her supremacy and retreated to a secluded spot in order to engage in deep meditation. Many devotees and sages came to that spot to have *darshan* of this Goddess of wealth. In response to their devotional requests, she agreed to reside there eternally as Arunakamalamahadevi. Realizing that living there in isolation would be improper, she prayed for the appearance of Lord Vishnu. The Lord was pleased and agreed to also reside there. Bhudevi and Neeladevi followed in His footsteps and reconciled with Sridevi. It was actually the desire of Lord Vishnu to bless His devotees at this spot, along with His Devis. Thus, this drama was enacted only to accomplish His desire.

Another piece of history of this place deals with Banasura. Many years ago he was the ruler of Mahishmathi and a zealous devotee of Lord Shiva. He had the strength of 1000 arms that adorned his shoulders. His daughter Usha was a devotee of Parvati, who prayed to the goddess for a suitable husband. That night after praying, she dreamed she met a prince of unparalleled charm, but after awaking, she did not know who he was. Her good friend Chitralekha knew the art of painting the images of all the eligible princes. When

Usha saw the portrait of Aniruddha, the grandson of Lord Krishna, she greatly blushed. Chitralekha then used her skills of conjuration to transport Aniruddha to the palace of Usha. There they merrily spent a few days together.

Banasura soon detected something was amiss and was infuriated to learn what was going on. Banasura took his army to find and crush Aniruddha, but Lord Krishna also brought His army to find His grandson. Then, due to the entreaties of Banasura, even Lord Shiva appeared to offer assistance. It looked as if Shiva and Krishna would engage in battle. But by Lord Krishna's power, Banasura lost his 1000 arms and was left with only two. After realizing his mistake in the matter, the marriage of Usha and Aniruddha was allowed to take place in grand style. The *Sthala* (or local) *Purana* relates that it was here at Tiruthangal where the extraordinary wedding took place. Thus, the images of Usha and Aniruddha are also found in the main shrine.

Ramesvaram is easy to reach after seeing Madurai and the surrounding area, where we can catch the early morning train for Ramesvaram. It is a relaxing ride (about six hours) as we head toward the coast. Ramesvaram is a tropical island surrounded by coral reefs and sandy beaches with coconut palms and tamarind trees. It is a major center of pilgrimage for both Vaishnavas and Shaivites. The Sri Ramanathaswamy temple is one of the most important in India. It is a massive complex with a number of shrines, holy wells, *gopurams*, and several long hallways, one reaching 4000 feet in length, the longest in the country. The halls are adorned with many large pillars, some of which are covered with scroll work, lotus designs, animals, and other figures, and colorfully painted medallions are on the ceilings.

According to legends, this temple was originally started by Lord Ramachandra. Lord Rāma had gone to Sri Lanka to rescue His wife, Sita, and engaged in a great battle during which He killed the demon Ravana. Afterward, He wanted to absolve Himself of the sin by installing a *lingam* at Ramesvaram. He sent His most trustworthy servant Hanuman to get a Shiva *lingam* from Mount Kailash, but Hanuman was delayed in his return. Since Shiva had to be worshiped by a certain time, Sita made a Shiva *lingam* (known as Sri

Ramanatha) out of sand. When Hanuman returned with a *linga*, he was disappointed and angry to find another *linga* already installed. To pacify Hanuman, Rama had the Hanumath *lingam* (known as Visvalingam) installed next to the Ramanatha *lingam*. Then He ordered that all worship should first go to the Visvalingam. So, in this complex the main shrines are for Visvalingam and the Sri Ramanatha *lingam*. It is now the seat of one of the 12 *jyotirlingas*. Thus, the worship here goes back many thousands of years.

The Ramesvaram temple is also where Sri Chaitanya Mahaprabhu found the *Kurma Purana*. Within it He found a verse stating that Ravana kidnapped an illusory Sita, and the real Sita was safely hidden by Agni. This information has greatly relieved many devotees of Sri Sri Sita-Rama.

The Channekeshvara temple at Belur (155 km from Mysore) is the only one of the remaining Hoysala temples that is still a functioning temple. This temple is over 800 years old, started in 1117, and was built entirely of green chlorite by Vishnuvardhana after his victory over the Chola armies. It is said to have taken nearly 103 years to complete it. The temple enshrines the beautiful, four-armed deity of Keshava, which is said to have been worshiped by Lord Brahma at his abode of Satyaloka. Later, King Indradyumna is said to have brought the Deity here and worshipped Him until he left this world, after which the Devas continued the worship until King Vishnuvardhana began the worship. The king discovered the Deity when he was traveling through the area and one of his servants took a bath and was cured of leprosy while bathing in the lake known as Vishnu Samudra, which is situated on the outskirts of town. Legend says that the lake appeared from a drop of nectar that fell from Garuda's pot. The king understood that this was a special place, which was confirmed when the Deity of Keshava appeared in the dreams of both King Vishnuvardhana and Ramanujacharya, telling them to build a temple for Him. Thereafter, as instructed, the king discovered the Deity at Chandra Drona Hill, from where he took the Deity to Sri Narayanapura and then on to Velapura, now known as Belur. The Deity of Chenna Keshava is four-armed, holding the disc and conch shell in the upper hands, and lotus and club in the lower.

One interesting thing is that there is a large pair of chappals in a glass case in the front *mandapam* hall. The local cobblers believe the Lord walks to Bababudangiri hill daily to visit Lakshmi who resides there. It is said that the Lord appears in the dreams of the cobblers when the chappals need replacing. They spread red kumkum on the ground so that His footprints appear when He walks through it. Then they prepare new chappals according to the size. This is all quite miraculous for most people, but is common in the pastimes of Sri Krishna.

At another place known as Kankroli, 18 kilometers north of Nathdwara, there is the temple of Lord Dwarkadisha, managed by the Vallabhacarya *sampradaya*. The legend is that the Deity came from Mathura where He was worshiped many thousands of years ago by the great devotee King Amburisha. The temple is located on the banks of the man-made lake of Raja Samand.

Many other examples could be given of the stories and legends of Deities that are found in various temples throughout India, or holy places where temples have been established thousands of years ago, that show how long ago the process of Deity worship has been going on. There are also many additional references in the Vedic texts themselves which show the importance of Deity worship from many thousands of years ago, some of which we will review next.

SCRIPTURAL REFERENCES TO DEITY WORSHIP

Even in the *Puranas*, for example, there are stories that include and relate the importance of worshiping Deities. For starters, in the *Bhagavata Purana* (4th Canto, 8th Chapter) there is the popular story of the great sage Narada Muni teaching Dhruva Maharaja the best way to become spiritually realized. Therein he explains the form of the Lord upon which to meditate and how to worship the Deity or Sri Murti of the Lord. The interesting thing here is that the *Bhagavata Purana* was composed by Srila Vyasadeva about 5,000 years ago, and the incident of Dhruva Maharaja is known to have taken place thousands of years before that. So, this gives some indication of how long Deity worship has been going on.

Narada Muni describes, "The Lord's form is always youthful. Every limb and every part of His body is properly formed, free from defect. His eyes and lips are pinkish like the rising sun. He is always prepared to give shelter to the surrendered souls, and anyone so fortunate as to look upon Him feels satisfaction. The Lord is always worthy to be the master of the surrendered soul, for He is the ocean of mercy. The Lord is further described as having the mark of Shrivatsa, or the sitting place of the goddess of fortune, and His bodily hue is deep bluish. The Lord is a person, He wears a garland of flowers, and He is eternally manifest with four hands, which hold [beginning from the lower left hand] a conchshell, disc, club, and lotus flower. The entire body of the Supreme Personality of Godhead, Vasudeva, is decorated. He wears a valuable jeweled helmet, necklaces and bracelets. His neck is adorned with the Kaustubha jewel, and He is dressed in yellow silk garments." (*Bhag.* 4.8.46-48)

This gives a little idea of the descriptions from Narada Muni to Dhruva Maharaja. Yet, he goes on to explain that yogis who meditate on this form very soon are freed from material contamination. The mantra *Om namo bhagavate vasudevaya* is also worthy of chanting in one's meditation. But the physical form [Deity] of the Lord should also be installed. Then Narada describes how the Deity should be worshiped and with what procedures and paraphernalia. He also says, "It is possible to worship a form of the Lord made of physical elements such as earth, water, pulp, wood, and metal. In the forest one can make a form with no more than earth and water and worship Him according to the previous instructions." (*Bhag.* 4.8.56) This shows some of the elements of which a Deity can be made. But a devotee who seriously engages in this process becomes blessed by the Lord according to whatever is his desire.

Furthermore, in the 11th Canto, Chapter 27 of the *Bhagavata Purana*, Lord Krishna explains to Uddhava the details of Deity worship, how it is important, the benefits of someone installing a Deity in the temple, maintaining it, or the harm that comes to one for dishonoring the Deity or the temples.

Therein, Uddhava relates that all the great sages, including Narada Muni, Srila Vyasadeva, and Brihaspati, have declared that such worship brings the greatest benefit possible in human life. The instructions for this process first emanated from the Lord Himself, and were thereafter also spoken by Lord Brahma to his sons, headed by Bhrigu, and by Lord Shiva to his wife, Parvati. Thus, according to the conclusion he was presenting, this method of worship is appropriate for all orders of society.

Then Lord Krishna begins to explain some of the important points of Deity worship to Uddhava. Some of what He relates are that a person should worship only after cleaning the body with water and the use of mantras. One may worship the Deity form, or a form on the ground, in fire, in the sun, in water, or within the worshiper's own heart, and offer the appropriate paraphernalia in loving devotion. The Deity form appears in eight varieties, such as in stone, wood, metal, earth, paint, sand, with jewels, or in the mind wherein the offerings are provided mentally. A Deity may be temporary or permanent, the latter of which, once installed, should never be sent away. The Deity may be cleaned or bathed, and, thereafter, once the devotee has purified himself and the items, offered the appropriate things according to the type of Deity it is.

"Even very opulent presentations do not satisfy Me if they are offered by non-devotees. But I am pleased by any insignificant offering made by My loving devotees, and I am certainly most pleased when nice presentations of fragrant oil, incense, flowers, and palatable foods are offered with love." (*Bhag*.11.27.18)

In this way, the instructions of Lord Krishna continue in how to care for the Deity and what is to be offered, by which a person can receive both material enjoyment and liberation. Afterwards, "Singing along with others, chanting loudly and dancing, acting out My transcendental pastimes, and hearing and telling stories about Me, the devotee should for some time absorb himself in such festivity.

"The devotee should offer homage to the Lord with all kinds of hymns and prayers, both from the *Puranas* and from other ancient scriptures, and also from ordinary traditions. Praying, 'O Lord, please be merciful to me!' he should fall down flat like a rod to offer his obeisances.

Placing his head at the feet of the Deity, he should then stand with folded hands before the Lord and pray, "O my Lord, please protect me, who am surrendered to You. I am most fearful of this

ocean of material existence, standing as I am in the mouth of death."
(*Bhag.*11.27.44-46)

In this way, Lord Krishna concludes: "By worshiping Me
through the various methods prescribed in the *Vedas* and *tantras*, one
will gain from Me his desired perfection in both this life and the next.
The devotee should more fully establish My Deity by solidly
constructing a temple, along with beautiful gardens. These gardens
should be set aside to provide flowers for the regular daily worship,
special Deity processions and holiday observances.

"One who offers the Deity gifts of land, markets, cities and
villages so that the regular daily worship and special festivals of the
Deity may go on continually will achieve opulence equal to My own.
By installing the Deity of the Lord, one becomes king of the entire
earth, by building a temple for the Lord one becomes ruler of the
three worlds, by worshiping and serving the Deity one goes to the
planet of Lord Brahma, and by performing all three of these activities,
one achieves a transcendental form like My own. But one who simply
engages in devotional service with no consideration of fruitive results
attains Me. Thus, whoever worships Me according to the process I
have described will ultimately attain pure devotional service unto
Me." (*Bhag.*11.27.49-53)

The process of Deity worship is so important and special to
the Lord, that He also gives a warning to anyone who may try to
impede in this process: "Anyone who steals the property of the
demigods or the brahmanas [priests], whether originally given to
them by himself or someone else, must live as a worm in stool for one
hundred million years. Not only the performer of the theft, but also
anyone who assists him, instigates the crime, or simply approves of
it must also share the reaction in the next life. According to their
degree of participation, they each must suffer a proportionate
consequence." (*Bhag.*11.27.54-55)

Also, Sukadeva Goswami, over 5,000 years ago, explained in
the *Srimad-Bhagavatam* the means for worshiping the physical Deity
of the Lord, starting with this prayer: "'My Lord Vishnu, full of six
opulences, You are the best of all enjoyers and the most powerful. O
husband of mother Lakshmi, I offer my respectful obeisances unto
You, who are accompanied by many associates, such as Vishvaksena.

I offer all the paraphernalia for worshiping You.' One should chant this mantra every day with great attention while worshiping Lord Vishnu with all paraphernalia, such as water for washing His feet, hands and mouth, and water for His bath. One must offer Him various presentations for His worship, such as garments, a sacred thread, ornaments, scents, flowers, incense, and lamps." (*Bhag*.6.19.7.)

He also emphasized the importance of worshiping the Deity of Lakshmi-Narayana, where he explains: "If one desires all opulences, his duty is to daily worship Lord Vishnu with His wife, Lakshmi. With great devotion one should worship Him according to the above-mentioned process. Lord Vishnu and the goddess of fortune are an immensely powerful combination. They are the bestowers of all benedictions and the sources of all good fortune. Therefore, the duty of everyone is to worship Lakshmi-Narayana." (*Bhag*.6.19.9)

One other example is in the popular story of Prahlada Maharaja and the Lord's half-lion avatar of Lord Narasimhadeva. Therein, Prahlada explains the nine processes of bhakti-yoga, devotional service, to the Lord. The verse is:

sri-prahrada uvacha
shravanam kirtanam vishnoh
smaranam pada-sevanam
archanam vandanam dasyam
sakhyam atma-nivedanam

"Prahlada Maharaja said: Hearing and chanting about the transcendental holy name, form, qualities, paraphernalia, and pastimes of Lord Vishnu, remembering them, serving the lotus feet of the Lord, offering the Lord respectful worship with sixteen types of paraphernalia, offering prayers to the Lord, becoming His servant, considering the Lord one's best friend, and surrendering everything unto Him–these nine processes are accepted as pure devotional service." (*Bhag*.7.5.23) In this verse, the word *archanam* means "offering the Lord respectful worship" in the form of the Deity, the *archa-vigraha*.

A further recommendation for engaging in Deity worship is found in the *Bhagavata Purana* on the occasion of the solar eclipse at Kurukshetra, when many sages gathered to participate during the time of Lord Krishna. Upon being questioned about the best way to become free from the karmic bondage to fruitive and sensual activities, they replied: "It has been definitely concluded that work is counteracted by engaging in Vedic sacrifices [rituals] as a means of worshiping Vishnu, the Lord of all sacrifices, with sincere faith. Learned authorities who see through the eye of scripture have demonstrated that this is the easiest method of subduing the agitated mind and attaining liberation, and that it is a sacred duty which brings joy to the heart. This is the most auspicious path for a religious householder of the twice-born [brahminical] orders–to selflessly worship the Personality of Godhead with wealth honestly obtained." (*Bhag.*10.84.35-37)

Many of these stories that we are relating herein are also repeated in other texts, such as the *Vishnu Purana*, *Padma Purana*, *Varaha* and *Brahma Puranas*, and others. So, they are not exclusive to the *Bhagavata Purana*, which shows how important they are.

The following verse also begins to show the process that is involved in worshiping the *archa-vigraha*, or the Deity form of the Lord: "One should worship the Deity along with each of the limbs of His transcendental body, His weapons such as the Sudarshan Chakra, His other bodily features and His personal associates. One should worship each of these transcendental aspects of the Lord by its own mantra and with offerings of water to wash the feet, scented water, water to wash the mouth, water for bathing, fine clothing and ornaments, fragrant oils, valuable necklaces, unbroken barleycorns, flower garlands, incense and lamps. Having thus completed the worship in all its aspects in accordance with the prescribed regulations, one should then honor the Deity of Lord Hari with prayers and offer obeisances to Him by bowing down." (*Bhag.* 11.3.52-53)

All in all, this shows that Deity worship has been a serious aspect of the Vedic process for spiritual development for many thousands of years. Thus, as it is further said, anyone who engages in the worship of the Deity in the temple is said to have reached the truth of studying all of the *Vedas*.

DIFFERENCE BETWEEN IDOL AND DEITY WORSHIP

What we have been describing is called, in certain cultures, such as the Abrahamic religions (Judaism, Christianity and Islam) idol worship, which immediately has the connotation of something bad, false, evil, wicked, and certainly misdirected, as if it will take one to hell. It can conjure in the mind something to do with pagan worship of the devil, or other aberrations as something being a false god. It is, however, most peculiar that none of these religions have, nor do they offer, a clear concept of what is God or what He looks like. But they seem to offer a clear conception of the imaginary idea of what is the devil or Satan. They cry against the process of Deity worship, when that has been outlined most precisely in the Vedic texts, but they cannot give a substantial description of God or the various ways in which He can be worshiped. Christianity is responsible for this more than any other sect.

There is certainly a difference between idol worship and worship of the Deity in the temple. So, let us briefly clarify this point. In this age of Kali-yuga, the worship of and desire for the almighty dollar is certainly a popular but easily recognized form of idol worship in this age. The idol that is worshiped and striven for is the dollar itself. And this extends itself in many ways and forms. Worship of a product of our imagination is also a form of idol worship, which should be avoided. We cannot make up just any form and expect suitable results from worshiping it. But we must understand that the authorized Deity is not someone's imagination, but is formed according to the precise descriptions in the Vedic texts, and is installed according to the exact processes as outlined therein as well. That is what makes the difference. It is similar to the authorized mailboxes set up by the government. If you put your mail in one of them, it will be picked up to be delivered to the address that is on your envelope. However, if you make up your own mailbox and put it on a street corner somewhere, the letter placed therein will go nowhere. Similarly, a pure devotee or *acharya* who is qualified to communicate with God is also qualified to install Him in the Deity form. This is also done through the prescribed Vedic rituals, such as the *prana prathistha* or installation ceremony. Then Krishna accepts that form as His expansion to receive service, prayers, obeisances, and worship from His devotees through this authorized means.

The thing to understand is that once the Deity in the temple has been established through the sacred rituals that call the Divinity to occupy the Deity, the Deity then becomes an expanded form of the Lord. Thus, by worshiping the *archa-vigraha* or Deity form of the Lord, one can approach the Lord who then accepts the service of a devotee by His omnipotent energy. The *archa-vigraha* of the Lord descends upon the request of the *acharyas*, the spiritual masters, and works as an expansion of the Lord in allowing us to view the spiritual form of God with material eyes, and in accepting the service of the devotees. Otherwise, for most people, it is very difficult to see that which is spiritual with material senses, at least until we are qualified with a spiritual consciousness. Thus, the Deity is also the Lord's causeless mercy on us.

Foolish people who have no spiritual perception, or no knowledge of spiritual scripture, consider that the Deity is merely made of material elements, and is, thus, something material, not spiritual. But they do not know or realize that the Lord, being the controller of both material and spiritual energies, can turn what is material into something spiritual, and what is spiritual into something material again. Thus, He can appear as both spiritual or material, but His spiritual nature is never compromised in any way. That is the difference, and that is what must be perceived. When a person begins to realize that, then the act of *darshan*, or seeing the Deity is not a mere exercise in respect and veneration, but it opens the relations between the devotee and God so that it becomes seeing the Deity and being seen by the Deity. There is a special reciprocation between the devotee and Divine which opens to a new level of experience, and new level of a loving devotional relationship. That is when the Deity is no longer mere stone, paint, or wood, jewels, etc. It is the Divine, vibrant with life that is revealed by the Infinite Supreme to the infinitesimal living being.

In many places, as we have seen in the previous section and will further uncover in later chapters, there are stories connected with particular Deities and various temples across India and beyond of how the Deity acted in various ways in reciprocation to the love of the devotee, or in other ways to show the supreme spiritual nature of the Lord in His Deity form. The Lord Jagannatha Deities in Jagannatha Puri, for example, is one such place with myriad pastimes that have taken place between Them and the devotees. Many of these are recorded and can be read and enjoyed, which show that such pastimes with the Deity, of which some people would call miracles, have continued from ancient times down to the present day.

In the Vedic tradition, there have been numerous spiritual authorities and *acharyas* who have attained high levels of realization, love of God, and relations with the Lord through the Deity. These include Ramanujacharya, Madhvacharya, Vallabhacharya, Sri Chaitanya, along with Saint Jnanadeva, Namadeva, Tulasidas, Meera Bai, Ekanatha, Tukaram, Ramadas, and many others who have pastimes with the Deity that have been recorded. Reading the biographies of such advanced devotees can be especially inspiring.

Even Sri Adi Shankaracharya had specific relations with the Deity in the temple. Some people may question how this could be since Shankaracharya was an impersonalist, one who accepts that God has no ultimate form but remains impersonal as in the Brahman effulgence. However, if we study a little of his history, we will see that he not only had special communications with the Deity of the Lord, but he also established Deities in various temples.

He was known for having installed a Shiva *linga* at his matha at Gokarna, worshiped the Deity at Ramesvaram, constructed the Kamakshiamam temple and installed the image of Devi therein at Kanchipuram, visited Tirupathi and recited *slokas* or verses that glorified the form of the Lord, Bhagavan Venkateshwara, from foot to head. He built the Sringeri Matha after having constructed a Sri Chakra on a rock and worshiped the image of Sarada Devi. He had also established a temple of Lord Krishna, his family Deity, at his birthplace of Kaladi for his mother, which you can still see today. He had also visited the Guruvayur temple many times. Near the end of his travels, Sri Shankara went to Badrinath where Lord Vishnu appeared to him and explained that His Murti or Deity form was in the Alakananda River, which should be taken out and established in a temple that Shankara was to build. Thereafter, Shankara had the Deity of Lord Vishnu, Badrinarayana, taken from the river and then constructed and consecrated a temple and installed the Narayana Deity therein. The *pujas* or worship ceremonies were established and Shankara brought suitable Brahmana priests from Kerala and appointed them the traditional temple priests after giving them proper training.

In this way, it is clear that Sri Shankara recommended and established Deity worship in various parts of India for the practice and preservation of Sanatana-dharma, and for the personal spiritual development of the people.

In conclusion, with the kind of evidence as provided above, the importance and the antiquity of temple Deity worship in the Vedic tradition cannot be denied.

CHAPTER TWO

Darshan and the Significance of Deity Worship

Deities, called *murtis* in Sanskrit, are an important part of Vedic temples and the Vedic tradition, but what is the significance of Deities and Deity worship? One thing to understand is that all the images of the Deities in the Vedic pantheon, as found in the temples, are made according to explicit details and instructions found in the Vedic texts called *Shilpa Shastras*. From these instructions we find the means to portray the proper stance, hand gestures, and other factors in the image of the Deity. In this way, Deities are not formed according to whim but in compliance to the scriptural regulations. Then they are installed in the temple in an elaborate ceremony known as *prana pratishta*, wherein the divine personalities are called to appear in the form of the Deity. Some of the Deities are demigods, while others, such as Krishna, Vishnu, Ramachandra, are of the Supreme Being.

Some people, however, do not believe that God has a form. But many verses in the *Puranas* and, particularly, the *Brahma-samhita* establish that the Supreme Being does have a specific form. These texts also describe His variegated features, which include His spiritual shape, characteristics, beauty, strength, intelligence, activities, etc. Therefore, it is considered that the authorized Deities of the Supreme that are shaped according to these descriptions provide a view of the personal form of God.

Those who have no knowledge of God or His form will certainly consider the temple Deities as idols. But this is the effect of their foolishness. They think that the Deities are simply the products of someone's imagination, or merely made of material elements. Of course, there are those who say that God has no form, spiritual or material, or that there is no Supreme Being. Others think that since God must be formless, they can imagine or worship any material form as God, or they regard any image as merely an external manifestation of the Supreme. But images of the demigods are not additional forms or representations of an impersonal God, nor are they equal to God. All such people who think in the above mentioned ways have resorted to their own imagination to reach such conclusions and are, therefore, idolaters. The imaginary images and opinions of God that are formed by those who have not properly learned about, seen, or realized God are indeed idols, and those who accept such images or opinions are certainly idolaters. This is because these images or opinions are based on ignorance and are not a likeness of His real form.

Nonetheless, God is described in the Vedic literature, which explains that God is *sat-chit-ananda vigraha*, meaning the form of complete spiritual essence, full of eternity, knowledge, and bliss, and is not material in any way. His body, soul, form, qualities, names, pastimes, etc., are all nondifferent and are of the same spiritual quality or energy. This form of God is not an idol designed from someone's imagination, but is the true form, even if He should descend into this material creation. And since the spiritual nature of God is absolute, He is nondifferent from His name or any other aspect of Himself. Thus, the name Krishna is an *avatara* or incarnation of Krishna in the form of sound. Similarly, His form in the temple is not merely a representation, but is also qualitatively the same as Krishna as the *archa-vigraha*, or the worshipable Deity form.

Some people may question that if the Deity is made from material elements, such as stone, marble, metal, wood, or paint, how can it be the spiritual form of God? The answer is given that since God is the source of all material and spiritual energies, material elements are also a form of God. Therefore, God can manifest as the Deity in the temple, though made of stone or other elements, since He can transform what is spiritual into material energy, and material energy back into spiritual energy. Thus, the Deity can easily be accepted as the Supreme since He can appear in any element as He chooses, whether it be stone, marble, wood, gold, silver, or paint on canvas. In this way, even though we may be unqualified to see God, who is beyond the perceptibility of our material senses, the living beings in this material creation are allowed to see and approach the Supreme through His *archa-vigraha* form as the worshipable Deity in the temple. This is considered His causeless mercy on the materially conditioned living beings that He would allow Himself to appear to humanity as a Deity to accept our worship and service.

In this manner, the Supreme Being gives Himself to His devotees so they can become absorbed in serving, remembering and meditating on Him. Thus, the Supreme comes to dwell in the temple to accept our worship and attract the eyes to concentrate and meditate on the Deity, and the temple becomes the spiritual abode on earth. In time, the body, mind and senses of the devotee become spiritualized by serving the Deity, and the Supreme becomes fully manifest to him or her. Worshiping the Deity of the Supreme and using one's senses in the process of bhakti-yoga, devotional service to the Supreme, provides a means for one's true essential spiritual nature to unfold. The devotee becomes spiritually realized and the Deity reveals His spiritual nature to the sincere souls according to their evolutionary spiritual development. This can continue to the level in which the Supreme Being in the form of the Deity engages in a personal relationship and performs reciprocal, loving pastimes with the devotee, as has previously taken place with other advanced individuals.

At this stage, *darshan* is not simply a matter of viewing the Deity in the temple, but to one who is spiritually realized it is a matter of experiencing the Deity and entering into a personal, reciprocal exchange with the Supreme Personality in the form of the Deity. At that stage, you may view the Deity, but the Deity also gazes at you, and then there is a spiritual exchange wherein the Deity begins to reveal His or Her personality to you. This is what separates those who are experienced from those who are not, or those who can delve into this spiritual exchange and those who may still be trying to figure it out. For those who have experienced such an exchange with the Supreme or His Deity, at this stage the worship of the Supreme Being in the Deity moves up to a whole different level, with no limits as to the spiritual love that can be shared between the devotee and the Deity.

CHAPTER THREE

Why God Reveals Himself to His Devotees

When it comes to the *jiva* or individual soul attracting the attention of the Supreme Being who is *atmarama* or completely self-satisfied, how is it possible? What would the infinitesimal soul have that the Supreme Being would want? Why would the Lord, the Absolute Truth, be attracted to anyone, even if they are advanced in doing austerities, yoga, *pranayama* or breath control, Vedic and spiritual studies, going on long and difficult pilgrimages, or anything else? How would that gain the attention from the Supreme Being?

The fact is that in so many places in the Vedic scriptures, Lord Krishna explains specifically that the only way to attain Him is through love and devotion, *bhakti*. That is the process of bhakti-yoga.

Lord Krishna explains, "It is not possible to attain Me through *jnana* (knowledge, contemplation, or mental speculation), yoga, renunciation, penance, study of scriptures, or the performance of duty in the same way in which it is possible to attain Me through *bhakti*." (*Bhagavata Purana* 11.4.21)

"The devotees are My heart and I am the heart of My devotees. They know nothing except Me. I also do not know anything except them." (*Bhagavata Purana* 9.4.68)

"Like one who has no freedom at all, I am completely under the subjection of My devotees, as if they always hold Me in their fist." (*Bhagavata Purana* 9.4.63)

In the *Bhagavad-gita*, one of the most important of all spiritual texts of India, Sri Krishna explains so many times that it is through *bhakti* that one can reach the ultimate perfection and know Krishna in full, such as in 18.55. On the other hand, the path to

understand and reach the formless aspect of God, which is highly
acclaimed by many, is still missing the means of attracting the
Supreme Being to us. The thing to realize is that such systems as
jnana-yoga, which consists of the attainment of spiritual knowledge
and discrimination between the material and spiritual, can lead to the
Brahman, or the formless and attributeless aspect of God. Karma
yoga or adopting all our actions into pious purposes, leads us to
heaven, as long as the good karma we have acquired does not run out.
Yoga and the system of *yamas* and *niyamas*, meaning the rules and
regulations of conduct and preparation for higher perception, or
pranayama and breath control, leads to the realizations of the
Paramatma or Supersoul within us all. But none of these by
themselves leads us to Bhagavan, the Supreme Person.

It is *bhakti* which purifies and spiritualizes both the mind and
senses and the intellect so that they can perceive the higher
dimensions in which the Absolute Truth exists. Sri Krishna says in
the *Srimad-Bhagavatam*, "Just as by the continuous application of the
eye-ointment the eyes become clean and can see clearly those things
that may be difficult to see, the constant reading of the sacred texts
that relate My pastimes, or listening to them, purify the heart and the
devotee is able to see Me, who is otherwise too subtle to be seen with
ordinary senses." (*Bhagavata Purana* 11.10.26)

In this way, it is the *bhakti* or love and devotional service, or
actions that are absorbed and performed in loving thoughts of Lord
Krishna, that creates the force of attraction of Lord Krishna towards
His devotee. Krishna is charmed by this loving devotion when it
resides in His devotee and gains more pleasure from it than from His
own natural blissful potency. As soon as the desire to serve Krishna
arises in the heart of the devotee, it generates a corresponding desire
in Him to relish that service. The more pure love is aroused in the
devotee for serving Krishna, the more Krishna wants to go there and
experience that loving attitude and engage in reciprocating with that
devotee. The intensity with which Krishna is drawn to that devotee is
reciprocal to the intensity of the devotee's *bhakti* or eagerness to
serve Krishna.

How can Krishna accept the devotee's service if He remains
on the transcendental plane and the devotee on the phenomenal if he

has no need for such service and feels neither thirst, hunger, heat or cold? The attraction of the devotee's loving service makes Him come down to the devotee's level in the form of Sri Vigraha, or the Deity form in the temple, and accept all its limitations in order to receive the offerings of food, drink, *arati* rituals, or clothes that are lovingly offered to Him by the devotees. In this way, the Deity actually begins to feel the hunger or thirst, or the need for the service offered by the devotees. Then the Lord in the Deity form relishes the love and service that is offered. This is also the grace of God for the devotee, which paves the way for the devotee to move forward in his or her spiritual progress to attain the spiritual realm of God.

This grace or mercy of God is first developed by *sadhana* or spiritual practice according to the principles of that practice for the devotee's purification, but such grace of God is over and beyond *sadhana* alone, but is dependent more on the love that is developed and offered to the Supreme. It is the warmth of that love from the devotee that causes the heart of Bhagavan to melt and flow toward the devotee in the form of grace.

This is why the Supreme Being will take up residence in the form of the Deity, and in this way turns what appears to be a material form into something that is spiritual and reciprocal to those who are devoted in a loving way that attracts the Lord to them. Then the Lord may reveal Himself by so many ways to show the devotee that He is accepting their service, or even in need of their service, or in dreams to help guide them in their service, and so many other ways. Through this means the Lord kindles and urges the love the devotees have for Him to even higher levels of expression, up to and including not being able to exist without engaging in their offerings of devotional service to the Supreme. When this happens, the devotees feel their life is empty without being able to continue their offerings to the Lord in the Deity form. This is only some of the ways the Lord actually inspires deeper levels of love within the devotee, which attracts Him all the more, from which the devotee also continues to become increasingly attracted to the Supreme.

Therefore, the exchange between the Lord in the form of the temple Deity and the service offered by the devotees invokes the same spiritual atmosphere as found in Lord Krishna's own supreme transcendental abode of Goloka Vrindavana. The Lord accepts the service of the devotee through His Deity form and inspires the devotees to service in deeper levels of love, which enlivens the Lord, which thus enlivens the devotees, like a spiritual competition of greater and greater levels of loving ecstasy for everyone. This is the epitome of loving relations for which the soul is always seeking. This is also why the Lord begins to reveal Himself to be the divine personality within the Deity, showing not only that the Deity is more than mere stone or material elements, but actually reciprocates with the devotee as the Supreme Person. No other process can draw or attract the Supreme Lord as this loving devotional service. There are many examples that have happened, and many that continue to happen throughout the world in the way and for the reasons we have described. What follows are just some of them. Many more examples could be included because they happen in many ways, but I hope this will be enough to convey the variety of such interactions between the Deities and their devotees.

CHAPTER FOUR

Stories of Deities and Their Reciprocation

Deities can be considered as another channel or portal through which the higher dimension or the Supreme Being directly reveals Himself to those in the material realm. Without understanding this, or without becoming qualified to perceive it, no one will actually realize the deeper character or nature that can be within the Deities, and the reciprocation with Them that can be attained. However, we know that there will be many who are simply too dull-headed to be able to comprehend this. In spite of all the explanations and information that is supplied, they will remain full of doubt and scepticism, believing or perceiving nothing but what can be viewed with their faulty material senses. Thus, the finer aspects of the spiritual realm will remain aloof from such people, and they will never fathom how the Deity of the Lord can show Himself or interact with those of us who are still residing in the material world but are on the spiritual path. So what follows are various examples of how the Deities have revealed Themselves to Their devotees in various ways.

Historically, there are numerous temples throughout India that are important, or that have significance in the way they were established and what parts were played in their development, or are related to events from ages ago that took place at the present location. And as we travel the length and breadth of India we can take note of the various temples wherein the Deities have exhibited activities with their devotees in various ways. These show that the Deity is not ordinary or mere stone or marble or wood, but is imbibed with personality of the Divine Being and can make what is material into that which is spiritual, and, thus, do whatever the Deity wants to do to reveal Himself or Herself to the devotees.

Furthermore, it has been my own experience that as you travel through India visiting these temples, there are still so many spiritual experiences that you can have if you are spiritually qualified and open to them. By that I mean if you are practicing a spiritual path as in a regular *sadhana*, and have developed some appreciation for what lies in the spiritual dimension and beyond mere sense perception, then you also become eligible to have reciprocation in many ways with the Deities of these temples, if the Deity so desires. There is nothing but whatever blockages we have in our own mind that excludes us from such experiences.

THE TEMPLES OF VRINDAVANA

Let us first start with the temples in Vrindavana, the land of Lord Krishna. To recognize the spiritual significance of the holy *dhams*, or places of spiritual energy, may not be so easy for neophytes. As I said earlier, in order to perceive the spiritual atmosphere in places like Vrindavan you have to receive the blessings of the resident devotees and become qualified so that Vrindavan reveals itself to you. An example of this was related to me by a friend. When he visited the holy place of Radha Kund which is near Vrindavana, he met an old *sadhu*, a saintly man who had retired from material life and was now living at Radha Kund. My friend asked the *sadhu* some questions and at first the man hesitantly explained that he did not work or attempt to maintain himself. He simply depended on Krishna and chanted the Lord's holy names at Radha Kund. How he got his food was that a small boy would come by and give him some food every day. The man explained that as a person becomes more and more spiritual, he will recognize the eternal atmosphere that pervades Vraja, especially at Radha Kund, and he will not feel the need to take so much care of the body. My friend then asked him if he could actually see the spiritual world or if he had ever seen Krishna at this holy place. The old man said he had not seen Krishna, but sometimes he could here the *gopis* talking with Krishna or discussing amongst themselves how Krishna looked and what He was doing.

My friend then asked the old *sadhu* how it was possible for him to perceive such things? The man then began talking quite readily and convincingly told my friend that Radha Kund was indeed the spiritual world; you simply had to remove your materialistic vision. Then the old man took my friend's hand and pushed it flat to the ground on the banks of the Radha Kund and said, "Just touch this land and you can feel the spiritual nature of it." My friend told me that at that moment a charge went up his arm from the ground and he could actually feel the difference, that this was indeed a spiritual place. But before my friend got the blessings of this sage, he could not really feel the difference. And that is what is necessary. Until you can actually perceive it, all you can do is to try to understand with your mind and imagine how Krishna performed so many pastimes here, and how this place is spiritual. But the actual realization of such things goes much further and much deeper than that. It is a matter of re-establishing your spiritual identity and connection with the spiritual realm. It is the reawakening of your spiritual consciousness and actually perceiving the subtle nature of spiritual reality. That is our real nature, our real home. It should not be so difficult to re-establish our connection with it. It is only a matter of freeing ourselves of lifetimes of material conditioning. And that is, essentially, what the spiritual path is all about. When you begin to rise above this material influence, the habitual thoughts patterns that have become so hard to resist, and you begin to see what you really are as a spiritual entity, then you can also begin to enter into the perception of spiritual reality and see that, actually, it is all around us. It is everywhere. It is what we are, and the Supreme Reality is only waiting for us to rise to that level of understanding and witnessing this spiritual truth. Even a glimpse of this reality will change our lives, and that is when we can become open to receiving the reciprocation with this Supreme Reality, some of which we will discuss now.

The Deities of Sri Sri Radha-Damodara that used to be in Vrindavana, but are now in Jaipur.

RADHA DAMODAR

There are many, many temples that have significant histories and pastimes related to them in the area of Mathura / Vrinavana, or what is called Vrajamandala. For example, in Vrindvana, there is the Radha-Damodar Mandir. The original Deities of Radha-Damodar were installed by Rupa Gosvami in 1542, but were later taken to Jaipur where they are now worshiped. The present Deities are considered equal to the original. There is also a stone or *shila* from Govardhana Hill in the temple that has an actual footprint of Krishna on it. Krishna personally appeared to Sanatana Gosvami to give him the *shila*. He told Sanatana that because he was having difficulty from old age he should stop his daily circumambulation of Govardhana Hill and simply circumambulate the *shila*. The footprint became part of the stone when Krishna stood on it and caused the stone to melt from the sweet sound of His flute playing. Now pilgrims circumambulate the temple four times, which is equal to walking once around the 15 mile path of Govardhana Hill. You can ask the *pujari* (priest) at the temple for Giriraja *darshan* and for a few rupees he will bring this Govardhana *shila* for you to see.

RADHA SYAMASUNDARA

Not far away is the Radha-Shyamasundara temple, which is one of the seven main temples of Vrindavan and has some very beautiful Deities. It was established by Shyamananda PrabhuShyamananda Prabhu who was a a very elevated *bhakta* and disciple of Sri Chaitanya Mahaprabhu. In fact, one time he saw Srimati Radharani, Lord Krishna's closest devotee. Shyamananda Prabhu would regularly clean the little forest area of Nidhibana and once happened to find an ankle bell. He thought it must be Radharani's since he knew Krishna and Radha often spent Their evenings there. This is because Their pastimes continue to go on there in the spiritual dimension, even thousands of years after They were known to have lived here.

When Radharani discovered one of Her ankle bells was

missing, she sent Lalita to find it. At Nidhibana, Lalita saw Shyamananda Prabhu and asked him if he had found an ankle bell. He said he had and asked if it was hers. Lalita said it belonged to her sister and asked to have it. Shyamananda said he would not give it to her but only to her sister. Lalita insisted that he give it to her, and Shyamananda continued to refuse. So Lalita returned to Radharani and Radha decided to personally go for the ankle bell Herself. Approaching Shyamananda, Radha asked for the ankle bell and he was happy to give it to Her. Radha, being pleased with his service, revealed Her identity to him and by impressing Her ankle bell into his forehead with Her hand personally gave him a *tiloka* mark. Later, the other devotees and *bhaktas* criticized him for wearing a new style of *tiloka*. But that night Srimati Radharani appeared to Jiva Gosvami in a dream and told him that She was the one who gave Shyamananda the *tiloka* mark. Then all the devotees went to Shyamananda to ask for forgiveness and accepted that he actually saw Srimati Radharani. This is another story signifying that the eternal pastimes of the spiritual realm are continually taking place in Vrindavan.

PISI MA AND HER DEITIES OF LORD CHAITANYA AND LORD NITYANANDA

Down a few doors from the temple of Bana-Khandi Mahadeva near Loi Bazaar in Vrindavana, around a few corners from the Radha Syamasundara Temple, is the little temple of Gaura-Nitai (Lord Caitanya and Lord Nityananda) of Pisi Ma Gosvamini. She belonged to the famous Mukhopadhyaya family, the landlords of Delagrama in the district of Nadiya in Bengal. Before Pisi Ma became a devotee of Gaura Nitai, she was known as Chandrashashi. Once she happened to go to Siuri and stay in a house near a temple in which the Gaura-Nitai Deities of Murari Gupta, an associate of Sri Chaitanya Mahaprabhu, were served by Balarama dasa Babaji, a *siddha* or perfected saint. She saw the beautiful images of Gaura-Nitai and developed motherly affection for Them. She also started offering Them khira, a sweet made from 40 kgs, of milk every day.

Once the Deities said to her in a dream, "Ma! We are hungry. We want to eat *khira* prepared by you." When she told Balarama dasa Babaji about this he said, "The scriptures forbid the cooking of food for the Deities by a person not duly initiated." Therefore, she got herself initiated by Balarama dasa Babaji and started offering *khira* prepared by herself to Gaura-Nitai. Gaura-Nitai were now very happy to have a mother who loved Them so much. But Chandrashashi was not to stay in Siuri for long. Gaura-Nitai knew this. They trembled at the very thought of her going away. One night she saw in a dream that both Gaura and Nitai were holding the loose end of her sari and saying "Ma! You do not go away from here. If you go, who will give us *khira* everyday? You are Our mother and We are your children. How can children live without the mother?"

Chandrashashi, like a good but helpless mother, caressed Them lovingly but pleaded her inability to stay on in Siuri indefinitely and asked Them to leave her sari. But They would not leave. In a tug of war that ensued, a piece of her sari was torn off and remained in the hand of Gauranga. When Chandrashashi woke up, she saw that a piece of her sari was actually torn off. Immediately she went to Balarama dasa Babaji and told him about it.

The day had just dawned and the door of the temple was closed. Balarama dasa Baba opened the door. Both he and Chandrashashi were surprised to see the torn off piece of the sari in the hand of Gauranga.

Chandrashashi was overwhelmed with a strong current of ecstatic love that in a moment swept away her attachment to home and all its glory and splendor. With determination never to go back she began to live in the temple and serve Gaura-Nitai with motherly affection. How could she do otherwise after finding children like Gaura-Nitai?

Chandrashashi was only twenty years old at this time. Her staying alone in the temple with Babaji aroused suspicion in the minds of people who began to talk slanderously about her and Babaji. This pained her very much. One night before going to sleep she wept before Gaura and Nitai and complained to Them of her plight.

That same night, Gaura-Nitai appeared to her in a dream and said, lovingly throwing their arms around her neck, "Ma! Let us go to Vrindavana."

So Chandrashashi and Balarama dasa Babaji took Them to Vrindavana, where they are now worshipped in a temple in Vanakhandi. Once in Vrindavana, the people began to call Chandrashashi Pisi Ma, meaning father's sister. (From *Experiences in Bhakti*, p. 70)

In this way, she renounced her family and all her wealth at the age of twenty and came to live in Vrindavana with Them. Pisi Ma served Gaura-Nitai as if They were her own children. However, when she became a hundred years old, it was no longer possible for her to continue her service to Them. So she deputed Sripada Gopeshvara Gosvami, a descendent of Lord Nityananda for the service. He was very dedicated and he served in the mood of a friend to the Deities. But Gaura Nitai were accustomed to the motherly affection of Pisi Ma and did not immediately adjust Themselves to the friendly attitude of Gopeshvara Gosvami. Pisi Ma would bathe Them in warm water, while Gopeshvara used cold water. So the Deities caught a cold.

Pisi Ma, who lived in a room upstairs, could tell something was wrong and learned about the cold the Deities were suffering from. So she came down to see Them and saw Their red eyes and phlegm flowing from Their noses. She wiped the phlegm with a corner of her sari and touched Their bodies, feeling that They had a fever. She called Gopeshvara Gosvami and told him, "What have you done? You have bathed Them in cold water and made Them ill. See what severe cold They have caught and how Their nose is running?"

As she said this, she showed Gopeshvara the corner of her sari stained with Gaura-Nitai's phlegm. But Gopeshvara did not believe this. So Pisi Ma in anger held the other corner of her sari near the nose of Gauranga and said, "Baba, sneeze a bit." Gaura sneezed and again phlegm came out of his nose, and the temple was filled with its supernatural aroma. Gopeshvara Gosvami, realizing the real position of Pisi Ma, fell down at her feet in penitence. (From *Experiences in Bhakti*, p. 32)

I will describe one final miracle with Pisi Ma and her Gaura-Nitai Deities that I know. When Pisi Ma gave her Gaura-Nitai Deities to Gopeshvara Gosvami he wanted to serve Them in the mood of a friend, called *sakhya-rasa*, but he said They were too small and looked more like little children, which was not appropriate for his mood. He told Pisi Ma that the small size of the Deities failed to arouse his friendly sentiment, thus he could not serve Them to his full satisfaction. Then, to solve this difficulty, Pisi Ma entered the temple, held the chins of Gaura-Nita with her hands and pulled Them upwards. The Deities allowed Themselves to be pulled and assumed Their present form, which is taller, as they are seen to this day in Their temple in Vrindavana.

RADHARAMANA

Another important temple nearby is the Radharamana Mandir, founded by Gopala Bhatta Gosvami. Gopala Bhatta had been worshiping a *shalagrama-shila*, which is Krishna or Vishnu in the form of a stone he had gotten while on pilgrimage in Nepal. These special *shalagrama-shila*s are found in the Gandaki River there. However, Gopala Bhatta longed to have a Deity of Krishna to worship and dress. Then one day in 1542 the Deity of Radharamana spontaneously manifested from the *shalagrama-shila*, thus fulfilling Gopala Bhatta Gosvami's desire. You can still see the stone or *shila* on the back of the Deity, from which He manifested Himself. This is one of those miracles of *bhakti*.

LOKANATHA GOSWAMI AND THE DEITY OF RADHAVINODA THAKURA

Lokanatha Gosvami was one of the closest associates of Sri Chaitanya Mahaprabhu, and was commissioned by Him to go to the area of Vrindavana to rediscover the holy places connected with the pastimes of Lord Krishna. Vraja-Vrindavana was at that time covered with forests. So he went from forest to forest looking for the necessary evidence. While he was engaged like this, his mind was set

The little Deity of Radharamana of Vrindavana that manifested from a shalagram-shila stone by the fervent prayers of Gopal Bhatta Goswami.

on Krishna and His pastimes, and he always shed tears in such remembrance.

Once when he was staying under a Tamala tree near Kishori Kund, a pond in the forest of Chatravana, a thought came to his mind. He thought if he had with him Sri Krishna Himself in the form of His *vigraha* or Deity form, he could serve and please Him so that He might also help him in his explorations. The moment he thought in this way, Krishna felt attracted towards him and became restless to receive his service. He thought of a clever way to reach him immediately in the form of the Deity. He went to Lokanatha Swami in the guise of a tribesman with his own image and said, "Maharaja, this is my Thakura (Deity) Radhavinoda. I have been serving Him since a long time ago. Now I have become old and cannot serve anymore. I am leaving Him with you. I shall be happy if you kindly serve Him."

This was like a bolt from the blue for Lokanatha. The benign Lord had responded to his desire and come to him of his own. Tears of love and gratitude streamed out of his eyes. He took the image, clung it close to his heart and was for some time lost within himself. On regaining outer consciousness, he looked all round for the man who had brought the Deity, but he was nowhere to be seen. Who was he and where had he gone after doing him that great favor? The thought was plaguing his mind when the Deity of Radhavinoda smiled and said, "Who could bring Me? I have brought Myself. I was lying in Kishori Kund nearby. Since you desired eagerly to serve Me, I have come. I have been forcibly drawn by your love. I could not resist the temptation of enjoying your loving service. I am very hungry. Give Me something to eat."

Radhavinoda remained with Lokanatha till the end. Lokanatha made a bag from the fibre of some plant, in which he carried Him wherever he went. Radhavinoda felt happier in it than even in His celestial abode in Vaikuntha or Goloka. It is said that He was of great assistance to Lokanatha in discovering His own pastime places, *lila-sthalis*. Narayana Bhatta Gosvami writes in his *Vraja-bhakti-vilasa* that Lokanatha Goswami discovered as many as 333 forests and places connected with the *lila* of Sri Krishna. (From *Experiences in Bhakti*, p. 54)

LALA BABU AND THE KRISHNA CHANDRAMA DEITY

Lala Babu was born in 1775 in great wealth. His grandfather Ganga Govinda Sinha was owner of a large state and the Governor of Bihar. He inherited the property of his grandfather, thus becoming the richest and most respected man in Eastern India of his time. But the spirit of *bhakti* always dwelt in his mind. Therefore, one day he renounced everything and moved to Vrindavana. That is when he built the beautiful Lala Babu temple in Vrindavana, which you can still see there. He installed beautiful Deities of Radha and Krishna. The name of the Krishna Deity was Sri Krishna Chandrama.

After the installation of the Deities a strange thought came to him and he asked the *pujari* priest to keep a small lump of butter on the head of Sri Krishna Chandrama. His idea was that if the butter actually melted, it would indicate if the Deity was really alive. If the Deity was alive, then the heat of the Deity would melt the butter.

The *pujari* did as asked, and after a little while the butter actually melted and flowed down the Deity's cheeks. The *pujari* and the other devotees in the temple began to cry aloud with tears of joy. Lala Babu also become so overwhelmed with *bhava*, ecstatic love for Krishna, that he fell on the ground unconscious. (From *Experiences in Bhakti*, p. 31)

BANKI BEHARI

The Banki Behari Mandir is one of the most popular temples of Vrindavan. Haridas Gosvami found the Deity of Banki Behari at the bottom of Visakha Kunda in Nidhiban after Haridas had a dream in which the Deity appeared to him and told him where to look. When you visit the temple of Banki Behari you will see that the curtain in front of the Deity is closed for a few seconds every minute. This is because the Deity once walked off the altar and out of the temple to follow a great devotee who had come for *darshan*. Apparently the devotee and Deity gazed at each other too long and the Deity became fond of the devotee and later walked off the altar to find him. When the temple priests found the Deity of Banki Behari missing from the

The beautiful Deity of Sri Syamasundara, made from black marble,
at the Krishna Balarama Mandir in Vrindavana

The beautiful Deity of Srimati Radharani who accompanies Sri Syamasundara at the Krishna Balarama Mandir in Vrindavana.

altar, they went out looking for Him. After finding Him in the forest of Vrindavana, they placed Him on the altar again but began closing the curtain at short intervals to keep the Deity from getting too attached to any of the visiting devotees. This tradition has continued ever since then.

MADANA GOPALA AND SANATANA GOSWAMI

The Madana Mohana temple, located on a hill near the old river bed of the Yamuna, was established by Sanatana Gosvami. This was one of the first temples erected after Sri Chaitanya's visit to Vrindavan. According to records, it was originally Sri Adwaitacharya who had discovered the Deity of Madana-Mohana in the hill, called Dwadashaditya. It is also said that the original Deity was fashioned by the architect of the demigods Vishwakarma, under the direction of King Pariksit's mother, Uttara, many years ago. The Deity was called Madana Gopala when He was under the care of Sri Adwaita. It was Sri Adwaita who later gave the Deity to a priest in Mathura named Purushottama Chaube.

Sanatana Gosvami was entrusted by Sri Chaitanya Mahaprabhu with the task of rediscovering the holy places in Vrindavana. He lived there on Aditya-tila on the bank of the Yamuna River. But he would go to Mathura for *madhukari*, begging from door to door for something to eat because there were few people in Vrindavana at that time. Once he happened to go to the house of Damodara Chaube. There he saw the beautiful image of the Deity of Madana Gopala. The priest had treated the Deity like one of his children and when Sanatana Gosvami saw this he criticized the priest for not following the many rules and regulations for Deity worship. Then in a dream Madana Mohan told Sanatana that He had been happy with the priest's spontaneous love, but now He was no longer happy with all these rules that were supposed to be followed.

Nonetheless, the Deity stole the heart of Sanatana and he was lost in *bhava-samadhi*, totally absorbed in ecstatic love thinking of the Deity. He wanted to offer his loving service to this Deity of Madana Gopala, but he tried to suppress his desire. Certainly, the

Chaube family would not give away their Deity to him. But even if they did, how would he get the means to serve Him as well as the Chaube family?

However, it was not possible for him to suppress this desire. It grew stronger all the time, and the Deity was in his mind always. He would go to the Chaube's house on the excuse of *madhukari* to get the *darshan* of Madana Gopala. Madana Gopala could not remain unaffected by the seed of *bhava* and *bhakti* that had sprouted in the heart of Sanatana, for it evoked a similar desire in the mind of Madana Gopala.

There was no end to Sanatana's happiness and astonishment when one day Chaube's wife, who had motherly affection for Madana Gopala and served Him lovingly, said to him in a sorrowful mood and with tears coursing down from her eyes, "Baba! From today you have to accept the responsibility of the service of Madana Gopala. Gopala has grown up and become restive and unmanageable. He does not want to remain under the protection of His mother. He asked me in a dream yesterday night to give Him to you. I have also become old and imbecile and cannot serve Him well. It is in His interest that I entrust Him to someone, who can serve Him well and with affection." Fortune smiled on Sanatana. He returned to his *kutir* (cottage) with the treasure of his heart.

At first Sanatana used to keep Madana Mohan in a tree because he had no where else to keep Him. Later, Sanatana built another hut of straw near his own as his temple in which he installed Madana Gopala. For offerings to His Deity, Sanatana still had to depend on doing *madhukari*, and from whatever flour he got he prepared *bati*. This was prepared by kneading flour, rolling it into balls and baking them on fire. He would then offer them to Madana Gopala with saltless and spiceless vegetable, prepared from leaves he collected in the forest. Madana Gopala somehow kept accepting and swallowing this fare for a few days, hesitating to complain about it. But one day he said to Sanatana in a dream, "Sanatana, I find it difficult to swallow this *bati* of flour and leaves boiled without salt. I have to push them down My throat forcibly. Why not give me some salt along with these?"

Tears trickled down from the eyes of Sanatana. In utter

helplessness he said in all humility with folded hands, "Prabhu! You know that Your humble servant is a recluse, without any wherewithal for your service. You ask for salt today. Tomorrow You may ask for molasses and then for *raj-bhoga* (a large royal offering of food). How shall I manage? I have been enjoined by Chaitanya Mahaprabhu to follow the ideal of a Vaishnava Vairagi (a Krishna devotee renunciant), who is supposed to not ask for anything from anyone and remain content with whatever he gets from *madhukari*. You know that in *madhukari* people give flour, but no salt."

Did Madana Gopala feel humiliated? Did He think of going back to the house of Damodara Chaube where He got better things to eat? No. Greedy persons do not mind humiliation. His greed was for the loving service of Sanatana was so great that He preferred to suffer humiliation and eat the poor and saltless food he gave rather than leave him. For Him the love behind the food he offered was more precious than the food itself. (Based on *Experiences in Bhakti*, p.56)

To continue the story, just then a rich merchant was taking a boat loaded with salt down the Yamuna River. By Krishna's will the boat became stuck in the shallow river. Madana Mohan then changed into a cowherd boy who led the merchant to Sanatana. Sanatana could do nothing to help the merchant, so the merchant prayed to Madana Mohan that if his boat became free he would sell his salt and return to use the money to build a nice temple for Sri Madana Mohan. After praying, the merchant returned to his boat and found that it was no longer stuck. When the merchant sold the salt, he returned to build the temple. So this is how the temple was erected. Later, this was the Deity from which Krishnadas Kaviraja got the inspiration to write the *Caitanya-caritamrta*.

Unfortunately, in 1670, due to the threat of fanatic Muslims, the original Radha-Madana Mohan Deities were moved to Jaipur, and then again moved to Karauli where a nice temple was built for them. *Pratibhuh* or replacement Deities were later installed in the Vrindavana temple. You can still see the *bhajan kutir*, or place of worship, of Sanatana Gosvami, along with a well said to have been dug by Krishna Himself for Sanatana's water. This shows the exquisite relations that the Deities of Krishna can display with His devotees.

The Deity of Madana Mohana as He now appears in Karauli

MADANA MOHANA IN KARAULI

After Sanatana Gosvami's Deity of Madana Gopala became Madana Mohana and was later moved from Vrindavana to Jaipur and then to Karauli to be protected from the Muslim invaders in 1730, the activities of the Deity continued.

Taja Khan, a person in the court of Karauli, was a devout Muslim. He lived in piety and went to the mosque every day to say his prayers. He spent most of his time in reading the Koran and meditating on God. The Muslims revered him as a true Muslim, and the Hindus as a pious man.

One day he was sent by the court to the temple of Madana Mohana to deliver a message to the Gosvami in the temple. Then he happened to see the Deity through a window in the temple. He was so struck by its beauty that he kept on looking at it for sometime. After he had delivered the message through the gatekeeper, he returned. But as he returned, he could not help but look again and again at Madana Mohana, and Madana Mohana looked back at him. He went back to the court and then went home and to the mosque. Wherever he went he found the image of Madana Mohana pursuing him in his mind until it was securely seated in the temple of his heart. He even forgot his prayers, Kalama and Koran. He only thought of Madana Mohana and kept his mind's eye always fixed on Him.

Taja Khan was born a Muslim and brought up in a culture which is averse to the Deity worship of the Hindus. How is it that the image of Madana Mohana captured his heart the moment he saw Him? It may be because of the pious *samskaras* or impressions from his past life which were revived the moment he saw Madana Mohana; or it may be that Madana Mohana Himself took to a liking for Taja Khan.

Taja Khan's heart, which was now full of love for Madana Mohana often spilt over in the forms of poems. He once sang in Urdu:

> Oh! How my heart yearns for Thee
> Unthwarted by hunger, thirst or sleep,
> O Madana Mohana! Give *darshan* to me.
> Each moment without Thy *darshan*

Appears like a *yuga* to me.
The sidelong glances thrill my heart.
Cast Thy glance but once at me.
Listen, O son of Nanda with moonlike face,
Taja Thy servant stands begging at Thy gate
for Thy *darshan* and Thy grace.

Taja Khan could not now remain long without looking at Madana Mohana. He tried to go and see Him every time the temple opened. He kept standing at the gate and looking at Him through the window. When the temple was closed, he peeped into the temple of his heart, of which the gates always remained open, and saw Madana Mohana sitting there, always looking and smiling at him.

The way of *bhakti* is sweet, yet at times beset with difficulties, trials and tribulations. Taja Khan also had to face them. His Muslim brethren came to know of his *bhakti* towards Madana Mohana. They declared him a Kafir (infidel) and excommunicated him. The Gosvami of the temple barred him from going to the temple and seeing Madana Mohana even from outside because he was a Muslim. One day he was going up the stairs of the temple when the gatekeeper pushed him down. He felt so much aggrieved that for three days he did not eat anything. He did not go to the court and remained lying at home, all the time weeping and sobbing in remembrance of Madana Mohana.

For three days Madana Mohana also remained cheerless without seeing him. One can imagine how deeply He felt his absence from what He did on the third day. Every night, according to the tradition in the temple, the *pujari* kept a silver *thala* or plate full of eatables near the bed of Madana Mohana when He went to sleep. That way the Deity may eat if He felt hungry. However, that day at midnight when everyone was asleep, Madana Mohana got up from the bed, took the plate of food, and in the guise of the attendant of the temple started towards the house of Taja Khan. On reaching the house, He knocked at the door. When Taja Khan opened the door, He extended the plate towards Taja Khan and said, "Gosvami has sent this sacred food (*prasada*) and said that you must come for *darshan* at the time of *shringar arati* tomorrow. No one will object to your coming. He has also said that when you go you should carry this plate with you."

Taja Khan was taken aback by this. He kept gazing at the young attendant who seemed to have a divine luster on his face. He took the plate from His hands and said, "Has Gosvami sent this? Has he really called me for the *darshan* of Madana Mohana?"

"Yes, yes, it is he who has sent it and he who has called you for *darshan*. Do come," said the attendant, who then went away.

All this was a mystery to Taja Khan. He was not sure to believe all this or not. But he was hungry and ate the food and then cleaned the plate. In the meantime, Madana Mohana said to Gosvamiji in a dream, "Taja Khan has not eaten since you pushed him away from the temple. I have given him the plate full of eatables that the *pujari* had kept for me, so that he may have something to eat. He will come for My *darshan* tomorrow. Do not prevent him."

In the morning when the pujari priest went to open the altar room, he was surprised to seer the silver plate missing. Trembling with fear he went to the Gosvamiji and said, "Maharaja! Thakura's (the Deity's) silver plate has been stolen. Believe me, I kept it with the eatables for Him near Thakura's bed at night and locked the door of the altar room from outside. Please do not suspect me."

"Do not worry," said the Gosvamiji. "The thief has confessed the theft. The plate will come."

Gosvamiji went to Maharaja Gopala Singhaji, who was the ruler of Karauli at the time, and reported everything to him. Maharaja was overwhelmed with *bhava* (ecstatic love) to hear about Madana Mohana's concern for His devotee and the trouble He took for his sake. He was also filled with love and veneration for Taja Khan, whose *bhakti* had subjugated Madana Mohana to that extent.

Taja Khan started for the temple with the plate in hand before the time of the *shringara arati*. But he was staggering on account of fear because he was still not sure that he was called by Gosvamiji. He apprehended that the young man who gave him the plate might have stolen it and given it to him for fear of being caught. He might even be one of the gang of his Muslim adversaries who might have hatched a plot against him so that he might be accused of the theft of the plate. As he reached the temple, he saw the Maharaja and Gosvamiji standing at the gate. He was all the more struck with fear. How could he think that they were standing there to honor and not to punish him? As he bent low to salute the Maharaja, the Maharaja came forward and embraced him. He said with tears in his eyes, "Taja Khan! You are blest. Madana Mohana has been so kind to you." Gosvamiji also embraced him and said, "Taja Khan! Forgive me for barring you from the *darshan* of Madana Mohana. I thought you did not deserve His *darshan* because you were a Muslim. Now I know that if there is anyone in Karauli who really deserves His *darshan*, that is you."

As the large number of people who had gathered on the scene saw the Maharaja and Gosvamiji embracing with love the poor person of the court of Karauli, they shouted with joy, "Taja Khan ki jaya!"

Taja Khan stood bewildered. The whole thing was still a mystery to him. "Why this sudden outburst of affection for me?" he thought. "How am I blest? How has Madana Mohana been kind to me?" Suddenly a wave crossed his mind. With a start he asked Gosvamiji, "Gosvamiji! Where is that servant whom you sent with the plate?"

Gosvamiji said, pointing towards Madana Mohana, "He sits there on the altar. But is He now the servant? He is the master of all, the creator and controller of the universe. Blessed are you because your love made Him the servant of the servant of His servant."

As Taja Khan heard this, his body trembled like a tree struck by storm. Tears streamed down from his eyes. His heart pained and he looked pityingly at Madana Mohana at the thought of the trouble He had taken for him.

After this, Taja Khan became so famous that it became difficult for him to live peacefully in seclusion. He left Karauli and no one knows where he went. But the people of Karauli still sing a song describing Madana Mohana as the servant who stole the *thala* (plate) for Taja. (Based on *Experiences in Bhakti* p.137)

RADHA-GOVINDAJI

The Radha-Govindaji temple of Vrindavana is another of the seven major temples of Vrindavan. It was established by Rupa Gosvami where he discovered the Deity. The original Deity of Sri

The Deities of Sri Sri Radha-Govinda, now in Jaipur

Govinda was installed in Vrindavana nearly 5000 years ago by the great grandson of Lord Krishna, King Vajranabha. The Deity had somehow become lost for many years but revealed where He was buried to Rupa Gosvami in a dream. Rupa Gosvami, using the directions he received from Govindaji in his dream, found the Deity and installed Him on the hill where he had found Govindaji in what became the Radha-Govindaji temple in Vrindavana 450 years ago in 1590.

The beautiful temple is made out of red sandstone. The temple is now only two storeys tall but once reached up to seven storeys, tall enough that it is said to have been visible all the way from Agra on a clear day. The Muslim fanatic Aurangzeb, doing his dirty work once again, dismantled the upper five storeys of the temple due to his envy. While his men were destroying the temple, there was a loud thunderous noise that shook the ground. This put fear into the hearts of the men and they immediately stopped and ran away. However, the Deities had already been moved. Due to fear of the Moghuls, before they arrived the devotees moved the original deities to Jaipur where today many pilgrims go to see them. So the temple now has *pratibhuh* deities, or representative expansions, of the original Radha-Govindaji that are worshiped.

When the Radha-Govindaji Deities were moved to Jaipur by Jai Singh, to protect Them from the Muslims, Sewai Jai Singh II first was residing in the building that later became the temple. It is explained that in a dream the king was kicked out of bed and was instructed that the building he was in was meant to be the residence of the Deities. When the king woke up on the floor next to his bed, he arranged to install the Deities in the present building and that his own palace would be across the park from the temple. This way he could watch the daily *aratis* to the Deities. In fact, Maharaja Jai Singh accepted spiritual initiation from Vrajananand Swami of the Ramanuja *sampradaya*.

Presently, this temple of Sri Sri Radha-Govindaji, located on the north side of the City Palace, is one of the most important of all temples in Jaipur. It is very opulent and the Deities are very beautiful. There is also a small Krishna Deity, Gaura-Govinda, that was worshiped by Kasiswara Pandit. This temple is extremely popular and is visited both morning and evening by hundreds of devotees. People will crowd around the altar to see the Deities, and after the *arati* the priests will hand out *maha-prasada* to the guests who try to scramble to get some. Devotees can also purchase offered food, *prasadam*, from the nearby stalls after the noon *arati*. In the early morning or evening there may be a lecture given by one of the local holy men, and afterward there will be the final *arati* for the day. Several other Deities from Vrindavana are also now situated in Jaipur, so that Jaipur is now considered part of Greater Vrajamandala.

GOVINDA DEVA AND THE GARDENER'S POMEGRANATE

As can be seen from the above description, the Deities of these Radha Govinda Deities have quite a lively history. To illustrate further, here is another story about Them.

After Maharaja Jai Singh built a new temple for Govinda Deva, he appointed Sri Govinda Charana Gosvami as the *pujari* priest in charge of the Deity's service. One morning when Gosvamiji opened the door of the altar-room for the early morning service of *mangala-arati*, he was surprised to see that the dress of Govinda was torn. It was not torn when the Deity was dressed the night before. The cut was long and straight, so it was not the work of a mouse. It actually looked like Govindaji had gone out somewhere in the night and torn His dress because it got entangled in something. Could Govindaji do that, even when the door was closed and locked from outside? No one else could have done that.

Gosvamiji did not take long to solve the mystery because he was not an ordinary priest, but a *siddha* saint. While in his *samadhi* meditation, Radharani appeared to him and said, "Last night both of Us went to a garden to pluck pomegranates. Lalaji (Krishna) had plucked only one when the gardener came to know. He ran after Us with his staff and We fled away. The pomegranate was green, but still Lalaji ate it all." Gosvamiji then looked around the altar of the Deity and was surprised to see the rind of the pomegranate and its seeds scattered all over.

Immediately Gosvamiji called the gardener. He asked him, "Did anyone go to your garden to pluck pomegranates last night?"

"Yes, Maharaja! A boy and a girl, both had gone. When I ran towards them with my staff, they fled."

"Oh, how fortunate you are, gardener, yet how unfortunate! Thakura (Krishna) and Thakurani (Radharani) Themselves went to your garden and you ran after them with your staff! Come and see what is lying here on the altar–the seeds of the unripe pomegranate They brought and ate."

The gardener was a great devotee of Govindaji. He went to the temple for the *darshan* of Govindaji at the time of every *arati*, unmindful of the sun, rain or storm. He had planted for the Govinda Deity several pomegranate trees in his garden. He would anxiously wait for the day when the trees would grow and bear the fruits so he could offer them to the Deities. The gardener would closely watch the trees, and his heart sprang with joy upon the sight of the flowers on the trees, which gradually turned into fruits. The fruits would take time to ripen, but Govinda did not have the patience to wait till then, He went to the garden anyway, plucked a green pomegranate and ate.

When Gosvamiji told the gardener about this pastime of Govinda and the gardener saw the seeds of the unripe pomegranate lying near the altar of Govinda, he was overwhelmed with emotion. Tears began to stream down from his eyes. Hairs stood on end. He kept looking at the Deity of Govinda. He could not say anything but "Govinda! Govinda!" and fell unconscious. On regaining consciousness he said, "Thakura! You came, but I could not recognize You, but I ran after You with my staff. I thought You were the children of some maid-servant of the palace and began to shower abuses on You. The trees and the pomegranates are Yours. They were planted for You. But You came like a thief, perhaps because You did not want that I should recognize You. What did You gain by concealing yourself from me, and from hearing all my abuses?"

The gardener did not know that Govinda enjoyed the abuses of a devotee even more than his praises. He did not know that He enjoyed to steal what belonged to a devotee more than to beg for it. When did He beg for the butter of the *gopis* (milk maids) of Vraja? He always stole it. He was, therefore, called the butter-thief

(*Makhana-chora*). A thief feels offended if you call him a thief, but this thief is different from others. He feels happy when you call Him a thief. That is the nature of Krishna's mischievous side when it is exhibited toward His devotees. That is His loving pastimes, to forget that He is the Supreme and to act like an ordinary little child.

When Maharaja Jai Singha came to know about the theft, he gave the gardener a piece of land in reward because he had grown trees of which the fruits Govinda could not help but steal. His descendants enjoy the yield of the land to this day. (Based partly on *Experiences in Bhakti* p. 80 and other sources)

UDUPI KRISHNA

The famous temple of Krishna in Udipi, established by Madhvacharya, is known for being an important religious center for teaching the Dvaita or Tatvavada philosophy, especially as presented by Madhvacharya. It is also known for that activities of the Deity here. One famous story is that of Kanakadasa, a staunch devotee of Lord Krishna. It was in the 16th century when Kanakadasa came to the temple to worship the Deity of Lord Krishna. However, he was not allowed to enter the temple because he was of a low caste, and at that time only the higher castes could go in the temple to offer worship. It did not upset him when he was not allowed inside, but he went to the side of the temple and prayed with intense devotion. The Deity of Lord Krishna was so pleased that He turned Himself in the direction of Kanakadasa and also made the wall to crack, forming a few holes in the wall so Kanakadasa could still see the Deity. In this way, the Deity reciprocated with His devotee and allowed Kanakadasa to see Him. Even today, it is the tradition that when pilgrims first come to the temple, they go to the side of the temple and view the Deity through the same hole in the wall, now known as Kanakakhind, before going inside the temple for a closer *darshan*. Nowadays, this Kanakakhind is decorated with colorful carvings depicting the ten main *avatars* of Vishnu.

CHAPTER FIVE

Deities in Other Areas of India

There are many other temples in the area of India that also have noteworthy stories to tell about the Deities that reside in them. For example, another place we want to see to the north of Kathmandu by 11 kilometers is Budhanilkantha at the foot of Shivapuri hill. Here we find the large Deity of sleeping Vishnu that was carved out of solid rock in the 11th century. One legend relates that the Deity was found when a farmer was tilling his field and saw blood oozing up from the ground after his plough struck something. The people dug into the ground and found the Deity. So there is no telling how old this Deity is. Many pilgrims now come here. We reach it by getting a bus near the National Theatre, a pleasant ride, but the bus stops often to pick up passengers. When the bus makes its final stop, the Deity is only a few minutes away. Anyone is allowed in the courtyard and can see the Deity, but the central pool, where the Deity is reclining on Seshanaga, is for Hindus only, which means those who are born Hindu. At the feet of Lord Vishnu, the devout chant their prayers and make offerings of rice, where the pigeons wait to eat it up. It is considered that the Deity sleeps continuously for four months in the rainy season, and in November there is a festival when thousands of devotees come to participate when the Deity wakes up.

JAGANNATHA MANDIR IN MAYAPUR

In Mayapur, about a four hour ride north of Kolkata, and a short ride away from the Chand Kazi *samadhi* by cycle ricksha, we turn down a dirt road. After a ten minute ride we arrive at the Mayapur Jagannatha Mandir in the village of Rajapur. The Deities here are very special and have revealed Themselves to the surrounding devotees in many ways.

A summary of the story about Them must be told. At the time of Lord Chaitanya, 500 years ago, there lived in Navadvipa a great Vaishnava named Jagadisha Ganguli. He would walk 600 miles to Puri each year to participate in the Ratha Yatra festival. But he was an old man and was affected with a disease that left him blind. Thereafter, his friends advised him not to attempt the long trip to Puri since it would be too dangerous.

Feeling despondent he thought of committing suicide. But Lord Jagannatha appeared to him in a dream and spoke to him one night and told him that while bathing in the Ganges the next day a log floating down the river would bump his head at which time his sight would be restored. Then he should take the log to a particular devotee carpenter and ask him to carve the Deity of Lord Jagannatha. When all this had happened, he took the log to the person to carve the Deities, but the carver was very hesitant to take up the task since he was a leper. Not only did he feel unqualified to do it, but it would also be extremely painful since his hands were diseased. Jagadisha insisted, however, explaining that Lord Jagannatha Himself had ordered this. So the carver began the work. To his surprise, as he worked he became cured of his leprosy.

Jagadisha brought the Jagannatha Deities to where They are now located and established Their worship. But after the disappearance of Jagadisha, the worship of the Deities decreased until They were forgotten. Over the years They became completely covered over by a termite mound. Centuries later the local villagers noticed a beautiful flower growing on the mound. When they went near it they could hear a voice saying, "Please bring me water, I'm thirsty."

Thus, some years ago, the villagers cleared away the dirt and found the Deities unharmed, even though They had been neglected for many years. In spite of the fact that the Deities were carved from wood and covered by a termite mound, They were still intact. The villagers then established a simple temple for Lord Jagannatha, Lord Balarama, and Lady Subhadra to resume worshiping Them.

Since that time the Deities had been worshiped by Phatik Chaterjee. But in 1979 the aging priest realized he would soon die.

*The Deities of (left to right) Lord Balarama, Lady Subhadra, and
Lord Jagannatha, in Mayapur.*

After much consideration he decided to make sure the Deities would
continue being properly worshipped by giving Them to the care of the
devotees of Iskcon. Phatik died shortly thereafter. Now the Deities
have a nice, new temple and are visited by many pilgrims from
around the world. Many come here to try the *maha-prasada* (food
preparations offered to the Deities) and relish its spiritual taste. The
scriptures state that Sri Ksetra, or Jagannatha Puri, is eternally
manifest in this area of Mayapur. Thus, one gets the same benefits of
visiting Jagannatha Puri by visiting this Jagannatha Mandir in
Mayapur. And here you get the special blessings of being allowed
into the temple to see the Deities, whereas in Puri itself, not everyone
is allowed entrance into the temple.

When we visit this Jagannatha temple we can see the Deities
in their nice new temple, which has an open *kirtana* hall in front of
Them. In front of the *kirtana* hall is a series of diorama displays
which relate the story of these Deities and how They were established
here. Behind the new temple is the old one where the Deities used to

stay. This is still used when the Deities play the part of getting colds and fever after Their bathing ceremony during Their annual Ratha Yatra celebration. Next to the road which is separated by a wall and in front of the old temple is the old *kalpavriksha* tree. It is said that Shiva and Parvati came here to perform austerities and still come here. Under this tree you will also see a Shiva *lingam* known as Kshetrapala. This *lingam* has revealed itself as Lord Shiva to the devotees here in a number of ways. So devotees come here to pray to Shiva and Parvati for *krishna-prema*, ecstatic love for Radha and Krishna.

Ever since the Jagannatha Deities were recovered, many people have continued to experience rare pastimes with Them. Many examples could be cited, but here are a few.

One devotee by the name of Jaimini Ghosh would serve the Deities regularly. But once he fell asleep outside the temple, and when he woke up, he found that he had somehow been transported to Jagannatha Puri during the time of the Rathayatra festival. So he enjoyed the festival there for several days. Then he remembered his parents and how they must be worried since they did not know where he was. However, he did not have the money for the fare back to his home in Rajapur. When he explained his situation to some local pandits, they said that if Lord Jagannatha brought him here, then go to the Deities and ask that He take you back. After going before Lord Jagannatha in Puri, he fell asleep at night and awoke to find himself back in Rajapur.

Another time there was an epidemic in the area and many were dying from it. Then one night Lord Jagannatha appeared in a dream to the *pujari* and explained how to make the proper medicine that would cure the people. Then the *pujari* told everyone so they could gather the ingredients, but one ingredient could not be found. Later in the day, one small boy who had never been seen before came to the *pujari's* wife and gave her a special branch from an herb. When the *pujari* saw it he was very happy because that was the last ingredient that they had been looking for. Then they made the medicine and everyone overcame the epidemic. From that day even the non-Hindus held great respect for Lord Jagannatha.

Another story that I had heard while visiting the Rajapur temple of Lord Jagannatha was when a ricksha driver came to the temple and ate some *maha-prasada* and took some with him for his friend, who was a Muslim. But when the driver offered his friend the *prasada*, the Muslim threw it on the ground saying that he does not eat food offered to idols. That night in a dream the Muslim saw Lord Balarama sitting on him and strangling him. As He was beating the man, Balarama asked, "Don't you know that My brother is worshiped by honoring *maha-prasadam*, and you threw it on the ground? I will kill you!" Subhadra was also in the dream saying "Kill him! Kill him!" But Lord Jagannatha merely laughed and said "No, no, no, don't kill him."

The next day the Muslim came to the temple and very humbly went before the Deities and offered respect to Lord Jagannatha and then asked for some *maha-prasada* while relating the story, but no *prasada* was available. "There must be something," the man pleaded. So the *pujari* found some scraps in a pot, and the Muslim gladly accepted it.

Once one of the Iskcon *pujaris* forgot to bring tulasi leaves for the offering to the Deities. Such leaves are important to include in each offering. He did not know what to do and did not want to leave the plate of food in case some children or an animal might come and spoil it. So he offered the food anyway while praying that the Lord would accept it without tulasi leaves. When he came back in time to do the *arati*, he saw there was a ten inch branch of tulasi leaves sticking up from the mound of rice.

Another time there was a Muslim girl who had very poor eyesight. In fact, it gradually got worse and the doctors said it was incurable. The family, having heard about the power of Lord Jagannatha, brought the girl before the Deities and she prayed to the Deities for help. Then after drinking the *caranamrita* or water that had been used to bathe the Deities for seven days her vision was miraculously cured. Even into her old age her eyesight was clear.

Another time a devotee, Sadhana Siddhi Prabhu and his family moved to the temple. One day his son Dalim came running to his mother crying hysterically. After she calmed the boy down he explained that he saw a beautiful broach on Lady Subhadra and wanted to take it for himself. But when he reached over to grab it, Lord Balarama swung His arm and slapped the boy across the face sending him tumbling out of the room.

There are many other pastimes that are told about these Deities, others you can read about in the book "The Pastimes and History of Lord Jagannatha in Rajapur" by Pankajanghri Dasa, published by Gouranga Releases, in Scotland.

SRILA BHAKTISIDDHANTA SARASVATI THAKUR IN MAYAPUR

There were many experiences that were had by Srila Bhaktisiddhanta Sarasvati Thakur, the spiritual master of His Divine Grace Srila A. C. Bhaktivedanta Swami Prabhupada, in the holy dham of Mayapur. As explained in the *Sri Bhaktisiddhanta Vaibava* (Volume 1, pages 61-2) by Bhakti Vikas Swami, in November of 1915, Srila Bhaktisiddhanta Sarasvati Thakur, had experienced the loss of his spiritual master, Srila Gaura Kishora dasa Babaji. This, along with other dilemmas he was facing in the Vaishnava devotee community after the disappearance of his father, Srila Bhaktivinoda Thakur, sixteen months earlier, made him feel disappointed and hopeless. He decided to keep to himself. With little food or sleep, he remained engaged in intense *bhajana* while wrestling with the problems.

Srila Bhaktisiddhanta's heart reverberated with Srila Bhaktivinoda's order that he continue with his service to Sri Chaitanya Mahaprabhu. And seeing the mass of people spoiling their valuable human lives, simply taking birth and then dying without information of or interest in the incomparable spiritual boons offered by Chaitanya Mahaprabhu, Sri Bhaktisiddhanta Sarasvati was unceasingly contemplating the need to preach. Yet, having experienced the kind of malicious opposition he would have to face for speaking the truth, he was reluctant to return to public life.

Then one day a gust of wind blew before him an extract from the *Sri Caitanya-caritamrita* which described how Lord Chaitanya instructed Sanatana Gosvami to compose transcendental literature, renovate the forgotten holy places, institute service to Lord Krishna, and propagate *bhakti-rasa*, the knowledge of the yoga of devotion. Taking this as a divine instruction, but feeling depressed and incapable, Sri Siddhanata Sarasvati pondered, "I have no public support, nor wealth, learning, or the intelligence required to awaken interest in the populace. How can I convey to the inhospitable world the pure teachings of Sri Chaitanya and establish the spiritual teachings as yearned by my gurus?"

Shortly afterward, one night at the Yogapitha, the place of Sri Chaitanya's birth, in a dreamlike revelation he saw approaching him from the east the Pancha-Tattva, consisting of the divine personalities of Sri Chaitanya, Sri Nityananda, Sri Advaitacharya, Sri Gadadhara, Srivasa, along with the six Gosvamis of Vrindavana, as well as Srila Jagannathaa dasa Babaji, Srila Bhaktivinoda Thakur, Srila Gaura Kishora dasa Babaji, and numerous other great devotees who had already left their physical forms. They told him:

"Sarasvati! Why are you worrying? Begin the task of establishing *shuddha-bhakti*, pure devotional service. Distribute the teachings of Lord Chaitanya universally. Expand the service to the transcendental name, holy place, and teachings of Lord Sri Chaitanya. With unbreached enthusiasm broadcast the perfection of *bhakti*, devotional yoga. We are eternally with you, ready to help. The support of unlimited people, immeasurable opulence, and boundless scholarship awaits the blessing to serve your mission. All will manifest when required. Come forward with full strength to distribute the message of Sri Chaitanya Mahaprabhu's *prema-dharma* throughout the globe. No worldly hindrance or menace will be able to obstruct this undertaking of yours. We are forever with you."

It was the next morning when the few young disciples he had gathered saw for the first time in many days his face refulgent in happiness. He related to them the vision he had seen. After that his determination to preach was fully rekindled and unretractable.

At another time, as told in *Sri Bhaktisiddhanta Vaibava* (Volume 1, page 388), while staying at the Yogapitha, Srila Bhaktisiddhanta came out of the Bhakti Vidya Bhavan at nearly two in the morning and called out, "Everyone, look! See over there! Gauranga (Sri Chaitanya) and Nitai (Lord Nityananda) are going on *sankirtana* (congregational singing of the Lord's holy names)! Follow Them! Follow Them! Come and see!" All of the devotees rushed out, but no one else could see Them. This is but an example of how he could perceive the spiritual dimension that appears in such holy *dhamas* and the spiritual activities that go on there.

Another time in the middle of the night, Srimat Tirtha Maharaja roused the devotees: "Get up! Look at what is going on!" Srila Bhaktisiddhanta Sarasvati also awoke and said, "Just see! The Pancha-Tattva are going by, chanting and performing *sankirtana*! Come, let us follow Them!" The devotees accompanied their guru out into the darkness, but only Srila Bhaktisiddhanta Sarasvati and Srimat Tirtha Maharaja could see Them. Such incidents were not uncommon in the pastimes of Srila Bhaktisiddhanta Sarasvati, especially in the holy place of Navadvipa *dhama* in Mayapur.

EKACHAKRA

The Birchandrapur side of Ekachakra, the birthplace of Sri Nityananda, can be reached from the central arch in the village. From there we go to the left and then make a quick right, and straight down the street through the houses we shortly arrive at the Bankim Raya temple. This temple was established by Nityananda's son, Virabhadra Gosai, to house Bankim Raya, the Deity that Sri Nityananda had found when He returned to Ekachakra after being absent for 30 years. When you get up to the altar you will see the small Krishna Deity in the center with Srimati Radharani on His left and Jahnava Devi on His right. It is said that Lord Nityananda left this world by entering into this Krishna Deity. There is also a Deity of Yogamaya on a separate throne to the right. The Radharani Deity was also found in Bhaddhapur about ½ mile to the west in the region of Birchandrapur. After that She was installed with Bankim Raya and called Bhaddhapurera, the mistress of Bhaddhapura.

SAKSI-GOPALA

About six miles from Puri is the Saksi-gopala temple, located between the Jagannatha Puri and Khurda Road Junction railway stations. A new station called Saksi-gopala is there where people get off to visit the temple. The Saksi-gopala Deity is the Gopala Deity who walked from Vrindavana to Vidyanagara, a town located 20 to 25 miles from Rajahmundry on the banks of the Godavari River. How this happened was that two brahmanas were traveling and visiting the holy places. One was poor and young and was serving the older and richer brahmana. The older one was so satisfied with the charitable service of the younger brahmana that he vowed in front of the Gopala Deity that he would give his daughter to the younger brahmana to be his wife. The younger brahmana protested, but the older one insisted. Later, when they returned home, the older brahmana hesitated to fulfill his promise due to pressure from his family who disagreed with the idea. The older brahmana then began to say he could not remember any such promise, while his son called the younger brahmana a liar and thief. There was some controversy about this between the two brahmanas and the younger one was concerned to uphold the dignity of the elder. In a meeting with the townspeople it was agreed that if the Deity Gopala came to testify as a witness, the older brahmana would give his daughter as promised.

The younger brahmana went all the way back to Vrindavana and related the situation to the Gopala Deity who at first said "I have never heard of a Deity walking from one place to another." The younger brahmana said, "That is true, but how is it that You are a Deity and talking to me now, although you are a Deity? Actually, you are Lord Krishna, the son of Maharaja Nanda. You are not a statue. For the sake of the old brahmana You can do something You have never done before." So, finally the Deity agreed to walk. He told the brahmana that He would follow him and that the sound of His ankle bells would indicate He was there, but if the brahmana turned around to look, He would walk no farther. So for 100 days they walked toward Vidyanagara, then the sound of the Deity's ankle bells ceased to be heard. The brahmana became worried and looked back, and the

Deity was standing there smiling. The brahmana went to gather the people of the town who were amazed to see the Deity. Then the older brahmana agreed to give his daughter in marriage as promised and a temple was built for the Deity. After the marriage ceremony the Deity of the Lord informed both brahmanas "You two have been My eternal servants birth after birth." That is how the Deity of the Lord became famous as Sakshi Gopala, the Deity who acted as a witness.

Later, the King of Orissa, Purusottama, was insulted by the King of Kataka (Cuttack). So Purusottama fought and defeated the King of Kataka and took charge of the city. He then brought the Gopalaji Deity from Vidyanagara to Kataka and built a temple there. The Deity also stayed in the Jagannatha temple for some time, but then was moved to a village about six miles from Puri, called Satyavadi. Some time after that a new temple was constructed where we find the Saksi-gopala Deity today. Though the temple does not allow foreigners inside, many people visit this temple with the understanding that whether the Supreme is in the spiritual strata or expands Himself in the material realm in the form of a stone Deity, He can change what is spiritual into material and vice versa whenever He wants. That is why a stone Deity can do what is considered miraculous things, like walk, talk, etc. Thus, it is accepted that the bona fide Deity of the Supreme is non-different from the Supreme Himself.

REMUNA

Remuna is a short distance from Balasore, south of Kolkata. Some pilgrims will want to stop at Balasore in order to take an hour long bus or auto-ricksha ride to Remuna. In Remuna is the temple of Ksira-cora-gopinatha, which is an important place of pilgrimage. This is the Deity who hid a pot of sweet rice (*ksira*) for His devotee Madhavendra Puri. The story is that once Madhavendra Puri, while visiting Vrindavana, was told in a dream by Krishna that a Deity of Gopala had been placed in a thick bush by a temple priest to keep Him hidden from the Muslim invaders. Gopala wanted Madhavendra Puri to find Him and establish a temple.

So Madhavendra Puri gathered the local residents and was able to find the Deity in the woods and built a temple. Later, in another dream the Deity told Madhavendra that He was still very hot from so many years of living outside and needed some sandalwood paste to help cool Him. So Madhavendra Puri traveled all the way to Jagannatha Puri to get some nice sandalwood to bring back to Vrindavana.

On his way, he stopped at the Remuna Gopinatha temple, which is known for a special kind of sweet rice, called *amrita-keli* that they offer to the Deity. He was attracted to the idea of learning how to make it the way the cooks prepare it there so he could make similar sweet rice for his own Gopala Deity. But thinking that he was offensive for wanting to taste the preparation that was to be offered to the Deity, he decided not to taste any at all. However, that night the Deity Gopinatha told the temple priest in a dream to wake up and find a pot of sweet rice that the Deity had hidden behind His dress and to give it to Madhavendra Puri. When the priest awoke and looked behind the Deity's dress, there was the pot of sweet rice. Then the priest went out and after calling the name of Madhavendra Puri found him and gave him the sweet rice. From that time the Gopinatha Deity at Remuna has been known as Ksira-cora-gopinatha, the Deity who stole the pot of condensed milk for His devotee.

Furthermore, after Madhavendra Puri had secured a large amount of sandalwood and was on his way back to Vrindavana, he again stopped at Remuna. Then the Gopala Deity in Vrindavana spoke to Madhavendra Puri in a dream telling him that he should simply turn the sandalwood into paste and offer it to the Gopinatha Deity at Remuna. Since Krishna as Gopinatha in Remuna or as Gopala in Vrindavana or wherever He might be are equally the same, offering the paste to Gopinatha would also cool Gopala in Vrindavana. Thus, Gopala relieved His devotee Madhavendra Puri from the task of bringing the heavy load such a great distance back to Vrindavana. So Madhavendra offered sandalwood paste every day to the Deity until all the sandalwood and camphor were gone. A few months later Madhavendra Puri left this world and his *samadhi* tomb is located in Remuna a few minutes away from the Ksira-cora-Gopinatha temple.

All pilgrims traveling through Orissa should stop to see the temple of Ksira-cora-gopinatha at Remuna, who stands with Deities of Govinda on His right and Lord Madana-Mohana on His left. Also, the *samadhi* tomb of Madhavendra Puri is a short distance from the temple.

In this way, we can see that the Krishna Deities of this region, such as Jagannatha, Saksi-gopala, and Ksira-cora-gopinatha, are very active Deities and display Their supernatural qualities in a way that attracts many pilgrims to the temples of this area.

Also within the compound of the Ksira-cora-gopinatha temple is the *samadhi* tomb of the great Vaishnava devotee Rasikananda. Rasikananda was an important disciple of Syamananda. He had also helped bring numerous writings of the Vrindavana Goswamis to Bengal. Actually, it was Rasikananda who had found the Gopinatha Deity in the nearby pond after Gopinatha had been placed there to keep Him hidden from the Muslim king. After that, Rasikananda renovated the temple after the previous one had been destroyed by Muslim invaders, which had been built by King Gajapati Maharaja Langula Deva.

All this is elaborated by Sri Kaisoranandadeva Goswami, a disciple of Rasikananda. He explains that it all started in Treta-yuga while Lord Ramachandra and Sita were living at Chitrakoot. They had taken shelter of the ashrama of some sages during a rain storm. There were many cows in the ashrama. This reminded Lord Rama of His pastimes as Lord Krishna, for which He carved some figures of those pastimes on a black rock. Sita wanted to see these figures. So upon Her request, He showed them to Her along with the Deity of Gopal that He had made to exhibit His form when He would again appear on earth. He showed this along with figures of Krishna's eight main *gopis* and four other maid-servants. Other scenes included Lord Balarama wrestling Mustika, Lord Krishna wrestling Chanura, along with twelve cows and a few other scenes. Pleased by this, Sita began to worship the Deity.

When Rama and Sita left Chitrakoot, Lord Brahma took up the worship of this Deity, all the way through to the age of Kali-yuga.

Lord Ramachandra and Sita had previously visited Remuna

when They were returning from Lanka after Lord Rama had killed the demon Ravana. They liked this place and Sita wanted to bathe in the Ganga. So Lord Rama shot seven arrows into the ground to bring up the Ganga River. That is now called Saptashara (seven arrows) in Remuna. That is where the *murti* of Shiva as Gadegadeshwara was installed. The image of Durga Devi is in the nearby temple of Ramacandi. Because Lord Rama felt pleasure (*ramana*) here, it became known as Remuna.

It was in the thirteenth century when King Langula Narasimhadeva from Orissa stopped at Chitrakoot during his travels and happened to see this Gopala Deity. He was amazed that no one seemed to be worshiping the lovely Deity, not knowing that Lord Brahma was still arriving everyday to do the *puja*. But that night the king had a dream in which the Deity of Gopala requested to be taken to a more inhabited place. So the king decided to take Him to Jagannatha Puri. However, while passing through Remuna, the Deity again appeared to the king in a dream and asked to be installed there. So the king arranged it. The queen noticed the eight principal *gopis* on the stone of the Deity, so she called Him Gopal.

Shortly after the time of Sri Chaitanya Mahaprabhu, there was a Muslim king who would go and smash the Deities in temples. People of Remuna heard he was coming there, so they took the Gopala Deity and hid Him in a pond three miles away. Being upset that he could not find the Gopala Deity, the Muslim king assaulted and partially broke the Ramacandi Durga Deity.

Later, the great devotee Rasikananda had a dream in which he was ordered to excavate the pond to recover the Deity of Gopinatha. After doing so, he built a temple for the Deity and established the worship. Later, when Rasikananda had made up his mind that it was time for him to leave this world, he entered the temple of Gopinatha and disappeared. Seven of his associates who had been performing *sankirtana* with Rasikananda also gave up their bodies to follow him into the spiritual realm when they became so spiritually distressed after hearing that Rasikananda had gone. Their *samadhi* tombs are also next to Rasikananda's in the temple courtyard.

ALALARNATHA

About 14 miles from Jagannatha Puri is the Alalarnatha temple at Brahmagiri. Lord Alalarnatha is a four-handed form of Lord Vishnu. Whenever the Jagannatha Deities in Puri would be removed from the altar before the Ratha-Yatra festival for two weeks, Sri Chaitanya would stay here. This is a temple where, at the end of the *kirtana* hall in front of a Deity of Sadbhuja (a form of the combination of Lord Krishna, Lord Rama, and Sri Chaitanya Mahapurabhu), there is a large stone slab with the imprint of Sri Chaitanya's body. Once when He fell onto the stone in an ecstatic trance, the stone melted leaving the imprint of Sri Chaitanya's body as we find it today.

Across from the Alalarnatha temple is another Gaudiya-Math temple that was established by Srila Bhaktisiddhanta. It is also here where we find a much smaller Alalarnatha Deity that was uncovered during excavations around the main Alalarnatha temple. How this Deity was found is that once when Srila Bhaktisiddhanta was staying at his temple, the priest at the Alalarnatha shrine had a dream in which the Lord came to him and said that He wanted to accept the worship of Srila Bhaktisiddhanta. Then the priest brought the small Alalarnatha Deity to Srila Bhaktisiddhanta who worshiped Him, and where the little Deity has remained since then.

YADAGIRI-GUTTA

Yadagiri-gutta is 60 kilometers northeast of Hyderabad, reached by bus (2 hours). Upon arrival at Yadagiri-gutta, you either walk a half-hour, or get an auto-rickshaw, or take another very crowded bus to the top of the hill.

Yadagiri was named after a sage named Yadava who performed heavy austerities to see Lord Vishnu as Narasimha. Being pleased with him, the Lord self-manifested and appeared in order to give him *darshan* in three forms: Jwala Narasimha, Gandabheranda Narasimha, and Yogananda Narasimha. Yadava begged for the Lord to remain on the hill in these forms. Thus, you have the Lakshmi-

Narasimhadeva temple on the hilltop with Deities of the Lord in all three forms embedded in stone in the main cave. Actually, it is a cave about 12 feet high by 30 feet long, located in back of the temple hall, by the rear pillar. You take a stairway down into the chamber and then toward the back. Jwala Narasimha is in the shape of a serpent, while Yogananda Narasimha appears sitting in meditation in a yoga pose. You will also see silver Deities of Lakshmi-Narasimha, which are quite striking in appearance and lends presence to the experience of seeing Them. To the right of the temple's main door is a Hanuman temple. You will see a long horizontal gap in the rock just below Hanuman. This is said to be where Gandabheranda Narasimha manifested. This is a very popular temple. It is said that any wish of the sincere devotee visiting this temple will be fulfilled. On weekends the lines to see the Deity can be very long. So it is best to go during the week. Plus, places to stay are few, therefore, consider taking a day trip from Hyderabad.

KANCHIPURAM

This is an important place with many temples to see, one of which is the large Vishnu temple for Varadaraja. It is one of the 108 Divya Desams, or holiest sites for Lord Vishnu. The Varadaraja temple is said to be on the site where Lord Brahma performed a fire (*yajna*) ritual to invoke Lord Vishnu. The central enclosure of the temple is supposed to conform to the raised altar that Brahma had used for the ritual. This shows how ancient this tradition is at this location. The temple is built on a small hill and has two high *gopurams* on the east and west sides of the temple compound that lead into the first enclosure, and a smaller gate leads into the inner enclosures. As you enter through the main gate, you will first see a separate *mandapa* hall which houses 96 elaborately carved columns that show many figures, such as dancers, animal riders, and scenes of the Vaishnava iconography. Some of them also produce musical tones when struck. There is some excellent sculptor work here. In the back of the hall is a *kund* or pond, called Ananta Thirtam. This is because Lord Ananta is said to have created it so He could recline in it and

observe the pastimes of Lord Varadaraja. There is also a story that
once during the summer's intense heat, the original Deity of Lord
Varadaraja felt overly hot and appeared to a priest in a dream
requesting to be put into the water. So they keep the Deity in a silver
chest in a shrine inside this pond. Every forty years the Deity is taken
out and worshiped in a grand way for forty-eight days. Around the
pond are several shrines, among which include a temple in which the
main Deity is Lord Narasimha on one side, and a Deity of the
Sudarshan chakra on the back. A shrine to Ramanujacharya is also
nearby.

THIRUATTUR (or THIRUVATTUR or THIRUVATTAR)

Thiruattur, about 50 kilometers south of Trivandrum, has the
Adi Keshava temple located near the banks of the Payasvini River.
Thiruattur is a small town, but many pilgrims stop in to see the
temple. The easiest way to visit Thiruattur and Suchindram is to take
a taxi from Kanyakumari. It is 46 kilometers from Kanyakumari, or
a 1 ½ hour taxi ride. You can also reach it by getting a bus from
Trivandrum going to Nagarcoil or Kanyakumari, and stopping at
Marthandum, and then get another bus to Thiruattur. Thiruattur is on
the Thoduvetti Kulasekharam Road. The temple is only about ten
minutes from the bus stop in a calm and isolated area.

The Adi Keshava temple has beautiful architecture but is not
as large as the one in Trivandrum, though the style is similar. The
architecture here, as with several other temples in Kanyakumari
district, resembles that of the temples of Kerala, using a combination
of wood and stone. This temple has been glorified by a decad of 11
verses composed by Nammalwar in the first millennium CE. It is an
important center of worship and is also referred to as Adi Anantam
and Dakshina Vaikuntham.

The legend behind this temple involves Lord Brahma. It is
described that once when Brahma wanted to have *darshan* of
MahaVishnu, he performed a penance, but he failed to perform it
properly in regard to the rules in the Agamas. Thus, from the
sacrificial fire came a demon named Kesha, along with his sister,

Keshi. They immediately had one thing in mind, and that was to mitigate their enormous appetites. Brahma granted them the blessing of long life and that they could go anywhere in the universe in search of prey. Then the demons went everywhere, subjecting even the virtuous and pious to fear and suffering. The great sages could no longer cope with the atrocities that were being committed and prayed to MahaVishnu to save the world from this terror. Upon hearing the prayers of the devout sages, MahaVishnu and Adisesha both descended to the Earth planet. A battle ensued and the demon was soon forced to give up his pride and surrender to the Lord. MahaVishnu ordered Adisesha to coil himself over the body of the Kesha demon. Then MahaVishnu reclined on Adisesha and, in this way, keeps the demon bound up, otherwise his influence would escape and again wreak havoc over the planet.

However, the demon's sister, Keshi, vowed vengeance for her brother. She is said to have taken the form of the Tamraparni River, and then made the Tamraparni River flood the land. MahaVishnu, however, directed Bhudevi, the Deity of the Earth planet, to raise the level of the land, thus ending the attempts of the river to immerse the area. Humbled by this course of events, the Tamraparni offered obeisances to the Lord and went around His abode, like a garland that wrapped the temple with water. The place where the river divided itself to form a circle is called "Moonattu Mugam" and "Kothai Pirali." And the place where the river circles around it is called Thiruattur.

Shiva is believed to have taken on 12 forms to witness the battle that went on between Vishnu and Kesi, and to worship Vishnu. A pilgrimage to all of the 12 main Shiva temples here is considered complete only after visiting this temple at Thiruattur.

The temple at Thiruattur is situated on a platform in a compound of 1 ½ acres. It is surrounded by a massive 30-foot tall wall. Nearby on three sides is the Tamraparni River and its tributaries. On the western side is the *ghat* where a dip is considered to relieve one of numerous sinful reactions.

The temple still maintains the old traditions and male members must wear a *dhoti*. Entrance with pants or trousers is not allowed. You enter the temple through the eastern doorway after climbing about 25 steps. The gate is a lovely structure of tiles and wood, typical of the Kerala style of architecture, but similar to the South Indian temple *gopurams*. From the entrance, one goes south to the shrine of Sri Butanatha. Next is a room in the southwest corner where we find Deities of Adikeshava, Devi, and Venkatachalapathi. Walking along the outer hallway, we reach the place of the copper flagstaff, the *dwajasthamba*. This was installed by Maharaja Mulam Tirunal of Travancore in 1895. Next we come to the Nalambalam, the circumambulatory passage around the sanctum (Sri Balippuram), which is a hall with 224 ornately carved granite pillars. These have lovely images of Deepalakshmis, which are the Lakshmis (the goddess of fortune) that carry the lamps. No two images are the same, each one differing in hairstyles or in positions.

In front of the sanctum is the Mukhamantap hall, which is shaped out of a single piece of black granite. This is three feet thick and 17 ½ by 15 feet long. It certainly shows the skill of which the stone carvers had during the day when this temple was built. The pillars nearby in the Balipeeta Mantap have life-size images that include Vishnu, Lakshmana, Indrajit, Venugopal, Nataraja, and Parvati, and even Brahma playing the veena, as well as others. There is also a shrine to Tiruvambadi Krishna. Additional shrines to Adi Kesava, Venkatachalapati, and Taayaar are also found. And the flag staff of copper was built by the Travancore royal family.

The sanctum faces west, although the main temple entrance is to the east. In this inner sanctum is the Deity of MahaVishnu who is 18 feet long and lies on Seshanaga. The Deity faces west as it is said that He is looking toward the Sri Padmanabhaswamy temple in Trivandrum. For a full *darshan*, the Deity must be viewed through three doors. The sanctum has been designed so that the rays of the setting sun illuminate the face of the Deity. MahaVishnu lets His left hand hang down. The hoods of Adisesha rising over the head of MahaVishnu can also be seen. The Deity is beautifully made out of a combination of ingredients that is known as Katusarkara yogam. This requires that the Deity is not washed with water, but the smaller or festival Deity is regularly worshiped, anointed, and dressed in ornaments and flowers. One man there told me the Deity was made of 16,108 *shalagram shilas*. This Deity is also accompanied by

Lakshmi and Bhudevi on either side. A separate shrine is found in which the Deity of Alambadi Krishna is located.

The *Padma Purana* describes the original temple at this location as having been built in Treta-yuga many thousands of years ago, originating before the Sri Padmanabhaswamy temple in Trivandrum. This temple is also one of the 108 Divya Desams (most holy places of Lord Vishnu) of the Vaishnavas. This is also the Krishna temple which Sri Chaitanya Mahaprabhu visited on His tour of South India and found a copy of the ancient *Brahma-samhita*. This has become an important text for all Vaishnavas.

According to the descriptions in "15 Vaishnava Temples of Tamil Nadu" by M. Rajagopalam, this temple is noted for particular miracles that have taken place here. One example is that in 1674, the Muslim vandals chose Thiruattur as one of their targets of attack. Queen Rani Umai Ammai Nachair, the ruler of this area, found herself unequal to the task of thwarting the attack. She went to the warrior-king Kerala Varma of Kottayam for support, but he was not hopeful for his chances at victory. He went to the Adikeshava temple and chanted fourteen verses to invoke the Lord to grant success for his endeavor. These verses are known as the *Bhakta Sangeerthanam* and are recited even today by the devotees. After chanting them, the ruler felt that a soldier clad in green armor had left the sanctum of the Lord. As the Muslim army approached, they were attacked by hoards of wasps. Their commander was stung to death. Thereafter, the demoralized forces ran for their lives and the attack was thwarted.

Another example is that in 1741 Marthanda Varma, the king of Travancore, was engaged in a bitter struggle with the Dutch at Colachel. Before embarking on the venture, he placed his sword at the feet of Adikeshava and sought His blessings. He emerged triumphant in the battle. Dilanoi, the Generalissimo of the Dutch forces, became his captive. Later, Dilanoi became an admirer of Marthanda Varma and was appointed the commander of the Travancore army.

In the eighteenth century the temple was again the target of the Muslim invaders. The army of the Nawab of Arcot desecrated the temple and defaced it of its ornaments. The smaller Utsava Deity was also captured and stored in a lumber room along with other articles.

The Deity, however, would appear on top of the pile everyday, pushing aside all the weights that were put on it. The perplexed Nawab had it chained down, boring two holes in the pedestal. At that time the Begum of the Nawab was afflicted with a disease. She was unable to withstand the excruciating pain. The physicians could do nothing about it. Then the Deity appeared to the Azhathi or guard of the temple, and told him to recover the small festival or *utsava* Deity. Explaining the greatness of the Lord, the Azhathi convinced the Nawab that the disease would be cured once the Deity was restored to its original place in the temple. The Nawab complied and was surprised that the disease in his Begum had disappeared. The Nawab repented for his blasphemous deeds and as a token of gratitude, he offered a pillow, crown, and a plate of gold. A special *puja* or worship was performed wherein a cap that is used to crown the Deity is fashioned like the Muslim head-dress. This was instituted by the Nawab and is still performed during the two annual Utsavams.

During the original *puja*, the Azhathi carrying the Deity placed it alongside the Shiva temple at a place called Thali and had a bath. On return he was dismayed to find the Deity could not be moved. The Maharaja came to know of this strange phenomenon and decided to take the Deity of Adikeshava to Thali every year for performing an *arati* worship. Only after this decision was made could the Deity be moved. This incident is commemorated every year during the Aippasi festival performed at Thali.

TRIVANDRUM (TIRUVANANDAPURAM)

Here we find the Sri Padmanabhaswamy temple, a large ornate structure built about 400 years ago. It is popular and busy. It is dedicated to Sri Vishnu as He reclines on His servant, Ananta or Adisesha. In fact, the name Trivandrum is short for Tiruvanandapuram, which means the abode of the serpent Anantha (Sesha). The temple is a Divya Desam, or one of the 108 most important temples to Lord Vishnu. The Deity of reclining

A print of the large Deity of Sri Padmanabhaswamy, a Vishnu Deity reclining on Seshanaga, who can be seen through three doors.

Vishnu in the sanctum is flanked on all sides by Sri Devi, Bhudevi, Niladevi, and different sages. From His navel sprouts a lotus on which is Lord Brahma. The Deity, made from 12,000 *shalagramas*, always had a black complexion, but He displays gold feet, hands, and crown. This place is mentioned in five of the *Puranas*, namely the *Padma, Skanda, Vayu, Varaha*, and *Brahmanda Puranas*.

The Deity is 20 feet long and lies in a compartment that has three doors in the front: one for His upper body, one showing His midsection, and another for His legs and feet. To get a full view, one has to do obeisances at all three doors. There are other shrines throughout the temple for Krishna, Narasimha, Subramanya, Ganesh, etc. It is open only to Hindus who must wear or rent a *dhoti* to go in. Men must remove their shirts as well. However, Westerners or white-skinned Hindus are forbidden to enter. Nonetheless, they can go in if they follow the procedure to get and sign a form stating their respect for Hinduism. But the procedure seems to change every few years.

Once in the temple, the halls are cavernous and there are beautifully carved columns and stone and woodwork. The hall that leads to the sanctum has 324 carved pillars. The Kulashekara Mandapam hall has 24 columns of excellent quality, four of which give musical sounds when tapped. It would be a photographer's delight if only you could take photos. But no cameras are allowed inside.

The origin of this temple is prehistoric. There is no clear evidence of when this temple was established or who had installed the Deity. However, according to the late Dr. L. A. Ravi Varma, a great historian, the original temple was built on the first day of Kali-yuga and is at least 5000 years old. From records such as *Grandahavali* and the *Ananthasayana Mahatmya*, it appears that the temple was constructed on the 950th day of Kali-yuga by the saint Divakar Muni from Tuludesh (Mangalore). The story in brief is that the sage was doing penance offering prayers to his favorite Deity. Suddenly, Lord MahaVishnu appeared before him as a little child. The saint became so fascinated and affectionate to the child that he could hardly think of anything else. He pleaded to the child not to leave him and it was agreed that the child would stay under certain conditions that there could be no misconduct by the sage. But one time the child began to chew on the sage's *shalagrama shilas* and acted in a most mischievous manner, and the sage got angry. Then the child said "If you want to see me, you must go to Ananthankadu," and immediately disappeared. Then the sage understood who the child was. The sage became so remorseful and began searching for the child. Finally, he saw the child disappear into the hollow of a big Alappa tree near the sea coast. The tree fell to the ground and assumed the shape of a huge reclining Vishnu, extending as much as 13 kilometers. His head was at the town of Tiruvallam (about 5 km from the present temple) and His feet at Trippapur (8 km in the opposite direction). Elated with joy, the sage prayed to the Lord to shorten His huge form so that it could be seen within the view of one's eyes. So the Lord shortened His form to equal three times the length of the sage's staff or dunda. The sage then began to happily worship this wooden form of the Lord.

Much later, after 1731 during some of the renovation of the temple, the Deity was replaced with a bed of 12,000 *shalagrama shilas* molded into the shape of the Deity with the help of kadukusarkara, which is a kind of mortar. This is the Deity that is worshiped to this day.

Thiruvananthapuram is mentioned in the *Bhagavata Purana* as Syanandoorapuram in descriptions of the pilgrimage of Lord Balarama. The temple has undergone various stages of renovation and reconstruction over the years, but is a sign of the great antiquity of Deity worship and the miracles that can be manifest through the Deities.

KARAMADAI

Karamadai is a significant Ranganatha temple. Karamadai is on the Coimbatore Mettupalayam highway about 23 kilometers from Coimbatore and just south of Mettupalayam, a good stop on our way to Mysore or Bangalore. The temple itself is not far from the bus station.

The temple is not the largest but occupies about one acre of land. The main eastern entrance has no tower, but the 40-feet tall *gopuram* rises over the northern entrance. However, they were building a new *gopuram* for the east entrance, which is probably finished now. This temple is rather modern, being constructed by Mr. Thiruvenkatavan Chettiar of Udagamandalam in 1944. Usually Vishnu is shown in detail only in standing, sitting, or reclining poses. However, the unique point about this temple is that the main Deity of Vishnu here shows Himself as a *linga* but wears the Vaishnava *tilak*. This is seen nowhere else. It is said that thousands of years ago Bhrihaspati performed an arduous penance and gained the favor of the Lord, who appeared in this way according to the sage's wishes. In other parts of the temple, there is the Deity of a two-armed form of Vishnu, Ranganayaki Thayar, whose charms attract numerous devotees. Also, the smaller *utsavar* or festival Deity shows Himself in a sitting posture. Other shrines are found in the temple and the outer walls of the sanctum have three niches with lovely images.

Sculptures of the Dasavatars of Vishnu also adorn the pillars of the main hallway, all of which reveal extraordinary craftsmanship.

In historic times, the area used to be dense forest that was filled with Karai trees. So the region was called Karaivana. Settlements of the Thottiar tribe were here, and their livelihood was raising cattle. One of them owned a cow that hardly gave any milk. So after watching it for a time, they found that it emptied its utter on a particular anthill. Thus, with utensils the tribesman tried to dig up the anthill but found that blood gushed forward. The main instigator of the dig also lost his eyesight and collapsed to the ground. His kinsmen sought advice from the spiritual preceptor, Vedavyasabhattar. Under his instruction, they built a temple to accommodate the Deity of the Lord that they found who appeared at this place of his own accord.

However, they could not understand who exactly this Svayambhumurti (self-manifesting Deity) was. Some felt that He was Lord Shiva, while others felt He was MahaVishnu. Then MahaVishnu appeared in the dream of a devotee named Pitchu Mandradiar and requested him to cover the Deity with sandal paste before dawn. While the sandal paste was being applied, Lord Vishnu gave *darshan* with the conch and disc in His hands, showing that He was certainly Vishnu.

Another interesting story is that during the time of the British rule, there was one man who was in charge of mapping the route for the railroad tracks. He prepared the tracks in such a way that it would be damaging for the temple and the water tank. Then in a dream, Lord Vishnu, mounted on a horse, appeared to him and hit him with a cane. The man then lost his eyesight. He repented for his irreverence to the Lord's temple and rearranged the route of the train tracks. Thereafter he regained his eyesight. As a token of gratitude, he gifted the temple with a horse *vahana* and arranged to re-lay the floor of the main shrines.

MELKOTE (or MALAKOTE or MAILKOTE)

Melkote is a small town 48 km north of Mysore. It has little in the way of accommodation, so it is best to be visited as a day trip from Mysore or Srirangapatnam. It is a sacred hill shrine with a temple of Madhvacharya, which has a Deity of Vishnu made of pure gold, standing 1 foot tall. Tiru Narayana is the name of the main temple. The Puranic names for Melkote are Vedadri (which means Veda Hill from which the *avatara* Dattatreya instructed his disciples), Narayanadri (the hill of Narayana), Yadavagiri (Yadu Hill where Krishna and Balarama of the Yadu dynasty worshiped the Lord in Dvapara-yuga), Tirunarayanapura (abode of Lord Vishnu), Bhulokavaikuntha (the realm of Vaikuntha on earth), Doddagarudanahalli (place of elite warriors), Doddagurugalahalli (place of great teachers, Ramanuja), Jnanamantapa (house of knowledge), Vaikunthavardhana Kshetra (the place which increases the population of Lord Vishnu's abode), Dakshina Badrikachalam (the southern Badrinatha), and Yathisailam.

The main Deities are said to have been given to Brahma by Lord Vishnu Himself. Tradition, as the *Naradiya Purana* explains, is that Lord Brahma once performed penance here, and Lord Narayana responded by coming to Melkote and assumed the form of a divine temple. Also, many thousands of years ago, Brahma gave one Deity to Sanatkumara. Lord Vishnu ordered Seshanaga to take the form of a hill at Melkote and wait for His arrival. Sanatkumara then installed the Deity and the temple complex in Bhuloka, planet Earth, at Melkote for the benefit of mankind. He later gave the Deity to Lord Rama, and Rama worshiped this Deity and later gave it to His son Kusha. Kusha also gave the Deity as his daughter's dowry when she married a prince of the Yadu dynasty.

When Lord Krishna appeared in the Yadu dynasty, He also worshiped this Deity. It was during this time that, while residing in the milk ocean, Lord Vishnu's diamond crown was stolen by Virocana, the son of Prahlada. Garuda killed Virocana and recovered the crown. However, while returning he saw Lord Krishna playing in Vrindavana with His friends. Garuda gave Lord Krishna the crown, known as Vajramukti. Krishna then gave the crown to the Deity Ramapriya.

When Lord Balarama, Krishna's brother, returned to Dwarka from one of His pilgrimages, he related to Lord Krishna that the Deity in Melkote was the same as their own family Deity. So they took the

The lovely and large Deity of Lord Vishnu, made of black stone but covered with jewels and golden hands, with rich paraphernalia, as found in the temple in Melkote, in South India.

Deity to Melkote and found no difference between the two Deities. So Krishna installed the Deity of Ramapriya in Melkote and the Yadu family regularly came there to worship that Deity.

Later, the story goes that in the 11th century, the Jain King Bittideva embraced Vaishnavism with the training and influence of Sri Ramanuja, and changed his name to Vishnuvardhana. However, at that time, because of the Muslim invaders, Narayanapuram was in ruins. Both the main Deity of Narayana and the smaller Deity of Ramapriya were lost. But Ramanuja had a vision in which Lord Vishnu showed him where the Deity could be found. Thus, he located the larger Deity among some Tulasi trees in an ant-hill in Yadavagiri, and then installed the Deity in the temple. As a service to his guru, Vishnuvardhana renovated the Tiru Narayana temple and built five shrines to Lord Vishnu known as the PanchaNarayana temples.

The smaller Vishnu Deity or Ramapriya had been given to a king who gave it to his daughter who became very attached to it as one of her dolls. Then later, when the sages wanted to install it in the temple, Ramanuja came to ask for it back. The king laughed and said, "I have so many dolls. You call it and if it comes, then you can have it." So he called it by name and the Deity practically flew into his arms. So then he took the Deity and it was also installed in the temple. The king's daughter, however, was so attached to it, but she was a Muslim and could not be allowed into the temple. Nonetheless, she also came to Melkote and there attained *mukti*, liberation. She is known as Beebu Nachiyar and is one of the saints of the temple. Her image is shown near the Deity.

Now when you go to this temple you can see that the main Deity of Lord Vishnu is black stone and shows Him holding a shanku (conch), chakra, and gadha (club). These are all covered in gold as are the Deity's hands, feet, chest, and crown. He also wears a colorful outfit, gold bead necklaces, bright garlands, and a large string of *shalagrama shilas* hang to His feet. So He is quite lovely to see. He is directly in front of you as you enter the temple and stands nearly five feet tall. The Deity of Ramapriya is in the Ranga Mandapam hall in front of the sanctum, on the right side of the entrance. This Deity was worshiped with great love by Lord Ramachandra. Shrines for the Deities of Vaikunthanatha, Chakrathu Alwar, and Anjaneya are on the *parakramas*, or walkways of the temple. And the Goddess Yadugiri Nachiyar (Lakshmi) and Kalyani Nachiyar have separate shrines in a *mandapam* hall of beautifully carved stone pillars in the back right corner of the complex.

On the hilltop at the other end of town, many steps up, is a temple to Lord Narasimha sitting in the Yoga position, so He is called Yoga Narasimha. He is nearly three feet tall and beautifully dressed and adorned in gold, with gold hands, feet, and crown with large flower garlands covering His chest. This Deity, according to the *Naradiya Purana*, is said to have been installed here thousands of years ago by Prahlada Maharaja, Narasimha's devotee and son of Hiranyakashipu. Beneath the temple is a small cave, just under the Deity, where Prahlada is said to have meditated. From this temple you can get a great view over Melkote. The town also has the Academy of Sanskrit Research, which has a large library of old Sanskrit manuscripts and palm leaves.

NATHDWARA

By taking short excursions away from Udaipur we can reach several other places we want to visit, such as Nathdwara, which is a very holy town. You can easily reach it by bus 48 kilometers northeast of Udaipur. It is the home of the famous Deity, Sri Nathji. Sri Nathji is Lord Krishna as He is depicted at the age of seven while He was in the act of lifting Govardhan Hill. Actually, Sri Nathji used to be called Gopalaji and had been worshiped near Vrindavana before being moved to Nathdwara. The story of how Gopalaji was discovered is described in the *Caitanya-caritamrita*. It was Srila Madhavendra Puri who came to Govardhan Hill and, after he went around the hill and began preparing for evening rest near Govinda Kund, a local cowherd boy visited him with a pot of milk. The beautiful boy made Srila Madhavendra Puri forget his hunger and thirst. Madhavendra asked the boy how he knew he was fasting, and the boy replied that he resided in this village and in his village no one fasts.

That night in a dream, the same boy came to Madhavendra

and lead him to a bush and explained that he was in the bush and suffered from severe cold, heat, rain, and wind. So Madhavendra was thus instructed by that boy to find the Deity with the help of the local villagers, who Madhavendra realized was Lord Krishna Himself. The Deity of Sri Gopalaji had been hidden in the bushes for some years and was discovered by Madhavendra. Then in a grand festival, the Deity was installed, using the water from Govinda Kund for the bathing ceremony. The Deity of Gopalaji stands with His left arm raised in the air in the pose Krishna took in the famous pastime of when He lifted Govardhan Hill as an umbrella to protect the local residents from the fierce rains sent by the demigod Indra.

Many people came to the place, named Jatipura (meaning "the home of the saint" in reference to Madhavendra Puri), to see and worship Gopalaji. A huge festival was started wherein the local residents brought offerings in large quantities of vegetables, fruits, grains, and many other preparations. This festival has continued in Jatipura to this day. Then a member of the royal family constructed a temple for the Deity on top of the hill.

After a few years, the Deity appeared in a dream and ordered Madhavendra to go to Jagannatha Puri to get sandalwood, which could be used to cool the Deity who was still feeling feverish from being in the ground for so many years. So Madhavendra left Jatipura to perform this service. When he arrived in Shantipur, near Mayapur, Sri Advaitacharya, an associate of Sri Chaitanya, asked him for initiation.

When Madhavendra arrived north of Jagannatha Puri, he stopped at the temple of Gopinatha in Remuna. The story of what happened there can be found in the descriptions of Remuna and the Kshira-cora-gopinatha Deity.

After Madhavendra Puri left this world, the worship of Lord Gopalaji at Jatipura was taken over by Srila Vallabhacarya, who had been initiated in the disciplic succession coming from Sri Vishnuswami, and taught the ideals of *pushti-marg*, or the worship of Lord Krishna in His childhood form. It was during this time that the Deity of Gopalaji started being called Sri Nathji by the devotees.

As with other Deities who were moved from Vrindavana to escape the fanatic Muslim Aurangzeb's destruction of Hindu temples,

Lord Sri Nathji was moved from His hilltop temple, which can still be seen on top of Govardhan Hill, to the land of Mewar from Jatipura. The Deity was first moved to Agra where the devotees kept Him in secret for six months, and then moved Him farther west. As the Deity was being moved, He reached a place where He could be moved no farther. The Maharana Sri Raj Singh accepted it as a sign from the Deity Himself, so he made arrangements to build a temple there. This is the place that later developed into the village of Nathdwara, which means the doorway to the Supreme Lord. This city has become one of the important pilgrimage places for the worshipers of Lord Krishna, especially for the followers of Vallabhacarya.

PANDHARPUR

Pandharpur is famous for its temple where the Deity of the Supreme Being is worshiped in His form named Vithobha, Panduranga, or Sri Vitthala. This place is called Bhu-Vaikuntha, the manifestation of the spiritual world on earth. The town is located along the Bhima River, which is considered as sacred as the Ganges and locally known as the Chandrabhaga. There is a short road with many shops on it that connects the temple of Sri Vitthala to the river. There are 14 bathing *ghats* along the river, but the main one is Maha Dvara Ghata.

How Lord Krishna came to Pandharpur many years ago is an example of how much affection the Lord can have on His devotees, as explained in the *Skanda* and *Padma Puranas*. It was while He was living in Dwaraka when Srimati Radharani, His consort from the village of Vrindavana, came to visit Him. But when Krishna's queen, Rukmini, saw how Krishna was dealing more intimately with Radharani than He had with her, Rukmini left Dwaraka and went to Dindirvana, a forest near Pandharpur. So Krishna went to find her, but His apology had no effect. So Krishna went to see one of His devotees at Pandharpur.

This most fortunate devotee was Pundarika, or Pundalika as He is known in Maharashtra. When Krishna saw him, he was engaged in taking care of his elderly parents. Pundarika, being a simple

Lord Vitthala, standing on the brick set there by His devotee
Pundarika, as found in Pandharpur

devotee, gave Krishna a brick to sit on and asked that He wait until he was finished serving his parents. So Krishna stood there waiting. In the mean time, Rukmini also joined Krishna and They both decided to stay in Pandharpur and accepted the forms of Deities. Now devotees from all over can come to Pandharpur and see Krishna as He stands on the same brick that was given to Him by Pundarika.

The present Vitthala temple complex faces east toward the river in the center of town. When you approach it from the west, you have to go around it to reach the entrance. There you find many flower vendors and little shops selling the usual assortment of holy paraphernalia, such as photos of the Deities, incense, beads, etc. In the very front of the temple on the steps is a brass bust of Namdev, the 13th century poet. People do not place their feet on the step on which the bust is located. It is stated that Namdev wanted to be on these steps in order to receive the dust of the feet of Vitthala's devotees. Out of respect, people come and worship the bust of Namdev, and you can watch as they offer incense, coconut, flowers, or place their heads on the base of the shrine.

Namdeva was a famous saint and devotee poet of Lord Vitthala. The most famous story about Namdeva is when he was a child and was instructed to care for the family Deity at home while his father was away. When it came time to offer a plate of food to the Lord on the altar, he expected the Deity literally to eat the whole offering, leaving nothing as *prasada*, or sacred food remnants. Namdeva waited to see if the Deity would eat, but after a while when the Deity still had not eaten, Namdeva went into the Deity room and insisted that if the Lord did not eat, he would smash his own head against the wall. Then the Deity ate the food, using His own hands to feed Himself. Of course, when his family returned, they expected to see the remnants from the Lord's offerings, so they did not believe Namdev when he told them that the Deity ate the offering. Only after they witnessed the Deity directly eating the offering were they convinced.

To enter the temple you must go through a gate on the left side to reach the doorway. Inside, you pass by a shrine to Lord Ganesh where you stop and pray that he removes any obstacles in your devotional service. The temple's courtyard is surrounded by a colonnade and in the middle are several altars and a pavilion for Garuda. Crossing the courtyard you will see the aisles where the queue of people line up to enter the temple's main hall. In the morning and on festival days the line of pilgrims can be very long. But in the evening of this ordinary day I was able to go right in with no waiting.

You enter the temple's sanctuary through two columned hallways. Embossed silver plates cover many of the 16 columns and doorways. Although most of the temple dates from the 17th century, parts of it date back to the 12th and 13th century. On either side of the door to the sanctuary are huge images of Jaya and Vijaya who guard the entrance to Vaikuntha, the spiritual world. I had prearranged to get some Deity *prasada*, so the temple assistants gave me some Deity flower garlands, *tulasi* leaves, a coconut and sugar sweets, which they instructed me to take home and distribute to my whole family. Then I went inside the sanctum to see the Deity of Lord Vitthala.

The Deity of Sri Vitthala is said to be 5,000 years old and self-manifested, without being carved or installed, as previously related. In the sanctuary you can see Lord Vitthala as He stands on a brick, slightly smiling, and dressed in fine, colorful garments, and wearing a *vaijayanti* garland. His hands are on His hips, His right holding a lotus flower and His left clutching a conchshell. He is a Deity of black stone, about three feet tall, and always attended by two or three priests. When you see Him, you grasp His ankles and place your head right on His feet. This is very special because in most temples you can only see the Deity from a distance, never being allowed on the altar or touching the Deity. However, in the morning hundreds and even thousands of pilgrims want to see Lord Vitthala, so you have to get there early, move fast, and put up with the crowd.

As everyone exits the hall, the devotees pray to the Lord to forgive any offenses they may have committed. They may also embrace the Garuda Stambha pillar and pray that Garuda will carry them back to the spiritual world at the end of their life. Also in the hall are additional shrines to Rama and Lakshmana, Kashi Viswanatha, and Kal Bhairava. Hanging from the ceiling near the hall's exit is the *Pandurangastakam*, the eight prayers composed by Shankaracarya that he wrote that glorify the qualities and devotees of the Lord when he visited Pandharpur. After we've seen Lord Vitthala, we circle around the main temple to the shrine of Srimati Rukmini, wife of Lord Vitthala, to offer our respects to her. As you wind your way through the halls and carved stone pillars of the temple, you see a few other shrines, such as one to Mahalakshmi, one to Vishnu or Balaji, another for Radha and Satyabhama, and so forth. Then you go out the back door facing town, which means you have to go around the temple and back to the entrance to get your shoes.

DWARAKA

Along with Badrinatha, Jagannatha Puri, and Ramesvaram, Dwaraka is one of India's four main holy places where, it is said, the spiritual realm overlaps into this material world. It is also said to be one of the Saptapuris, or seven holy places, which also includes Ayodhya, Mathura, Haridwara, Kashi (Varanasi), Ujjain, and Kanchipuram. Shankaracharya established one of his four *mutts* or centers here, and even Ramanujacharya and Madhavacharya came here on pilgrimage. Dwaraka is the remains of Krishna's capital city, which He established around 3000 BCE. It was one of the most developed and advanced cities anywhere. Descriptions of it are found in many Vedic texts, including the *Mahabharata, Bhagavata Purana, Vishnu Purana, Vayu Purana, Harivamsha*, and in 44 chapters of the *Skanda Purana*. It is described as having been full of flower gardens and fruit trees, along with beautiful singing birds and peacocks. The lakes were full of swans and lilies and lotus flowers. The buildings were also beautiful and bedecked with jewels. There were temples, assembly halls, residential homes, and as many as 900,000 palaces. While Lord Krishna lived here, the people of the town would often see Him. By local tradition, the present people of Dwaraka are considered to be family descendants of Lord Krishna, or members of the Yadu dynasty.

Dwaraka existed for nearly 100 years while Krishna lived here. This is where He appeared with 16,108 palaces for 16,108 queens. Although the city came under attack from local warlords, they could never conquer Dwaraka. When Lord Krishna was making final arrangements to depart from this world, when He left His capital the island fortress was covered by the sea, as Krishna said it would be. Presently, major excavations and archeological digs have uncovered varieties of artifacts that give evidence for the location and advanced nature of the city. On shore digs, conducted by the Deccan College of Pune, they found evidence of a settlement dating back to the first century. Further findings brought forth evidence that a city certainly could have been existing there from as long ago as 5000 years.

Offshore excavations, started in 1981 by the National Institute of Oceanography, brought forth evidence of a number of things. The sea level at Dwaraka was 60 yards lower 5000 years ago. A large fortification was found under the water. Other findings include pottery, bronze statues, terra cotta beads, and so on. The dates of some of the finds go back to the Harrapan Age.

The Times of India News Service also released an article on April 7, 1997, called *Krishna's Dwarka May Not be a Myth*. In the article, Mr. S. R. Rao, who heads the Dwaraka underwater excavation project and is a consultant to the Marine Archaeology Centre of the National Institute of Oceanography in Goa, remarked on some of the findings. The remains of three temples and a township on the seashore near today's Dwaraka compare well with descriptions of Dwaraka found in the *Mahabharata* and the *Harivamsha*. Another major township was also found nearly 30 kilometers away at a depth of 30 feet, spread over a four-kilometer area near the island of Beyt Dwaraka during underwater excavation. Mr. Rao identified Beyt Dwaraka as Kusasthali where the first town of Dwaraka was built under the direction of Lord Krishna as described in the *Mahabharata*. Excavations on the island reveal that civilization was active here as far back as the Harappan culture in the 2nd millennium B.C.E.

The findings they have made concerning ancient Dwaraka make it clear that the stories in the ancient Vedic texts, such as the *Mahabharata* and the *Puranas*, are not mere myths or fables. Dwaraka was a highly sophisticated and well organized city. Remnants of the wealth of the old town still affects life in Dwaraka today since gold fragments wash up on shore. More excavations were scheduled to begin at the end of 1997.

The main temple here for Lord Dwarakadisha is the center of attention in Dwaraka and many people have had various spiritual experiences here in relation to the Deity, including myself.

When we find the temple, we will make our way through a high archway and into the temple courtyard. The main temple is said to be 5,000 years old and built in one day by Visvakarma, architect of the demigods. However, most of the present day temple is said to have been built in the 16th century, but there are parts of the sanctuary walls that date from the 12th century, and the temple sanctum is said to date back at least 2500 years. It is supported by 72 pillars and reaches up to 235 feet tall. The temple is covered by ornate stone carvings, columns, and ornamentation. Like many temples in India, no photography is allowed inside. But once seeing it, the beauty of the place will stay with you for a long time. It is certainly a temple you will remember.

The temple is visited by many hundreds of pilgrims, local as well as from all over India. As you enter it, you first notice the smell of incense and the hum of the pilgrims chanting *mantras* and prayers. As you look around, the ceilings have many beautiful paintings of the pastimes of the Lord based on the descriptions in the *Puranas*. The floor is made of pink and black marble that is set in lovely patterns. The Deity of Dwarakadish is in the central shrine and has four hands. He represents the four-armed form of Vishnu called Trivikrama. This Deity is very old and is mentioned in the *Varaha Purana,* and He is worshiped with much opulence and reverence.

To see Lord Dwarakadish, you can stand in the central viewing area with the growing crowd of devotees. One side is for men, the other side for women, and the back is for everyone. When the curtain opens behind a silver doorway, the Lord is revealed in His beautiful four-armed form and the *arati* begins. Lord Dwarakadish stands five feet tall and is dressed in colorful clothes and beautiful gold, silver, and jewels. Around the Deity are priests who sing Sanskrit verses that relate the glories, characteristics, and pastimes of the Supreme Being. Above the altar are two-winged angels or Gandharvas who help protect the Deity. The priest then begins to offer such articles as ghee lamps, incense, and chamara fan. Everyone gazes at the Deity with the utmost respect. Some chant prayers and sing while others are very quiet in spiritual contemplation.

As you go around the complex, you will see other shrines, all of which contain a myriad of deities of demigods and goddesses, and various forms of Lord Vishnu and Krishna and Their consorts. All of Them are said to be very old. To the right of the main Deity is a small temple of Lord Balarama, Krishna's elder brother. To the left of the main temple is a smaller temple with a large deity of Pradyumna and a small deity of Anirudha, Krishna's son and grandson. Across from this is another temple of Purushottama (Vishnu). Another temple dedicated to Shiva as Kuseswara Mahadeva is next to this. Directly across from the main temple is a small temple for Devaki, Krishna's mother. And next to that is another for Veni-madhava (Vishnu). Once you visit these temples you can go behind the main temple to a rectangular building that has several altars around the sides with the Deities of Radhika, Jambavati, Satyabhama, Lakshmi, Sarasvati, and Lakshmi-Narayana. Seeing the temple at night is also very beautiful because it is lit up very brightly with many spotlights. Many people visit at this time as an uplifting way to end the day.

There are also other significant temples here, a few of which we will note. One is the Nageshwar Mahadev temple, which contains one of the 12 Shiva *jyotirlingas* (self-manifesting *lingas*) in an underground chamber. It is on the route from Dwarka to the Beyt Dwarka island. The *Shiva Purana* explains that the Nageshwar temple is in a place called Darukavan.

One legend connected with this temple is that a devotee named Supriya was attacked by the demon Daruka who imprisoned him and several others at his capital Darukavan, where he resided with his wife, Daruki. But Lord Shiva appeared as the *jyotirlingam* and destroyed the demon with the weapon known as the Pasupatastram.

Another legend is that Shiva, being sad over the death of his wife Sati, lived at Darukavan for some time in the guise of a sage. Darukavan was a land of snakes, and they cursed him to become a *linga* when their wives were enchanted by him. They were not aware of who he was. From the curse of the nagas, the *linga* was cast into the *kund* (water pool) and came to be known as the Nageshwara *jyotirlinga*. This *linga* was installed here in Dvapara-yuga when the

Pandavas found this unique form of Shiva. Lord Krishna told them it was Bholenath's (Shiva's) *jyotirlinga*, and that its worship will benefit the world. To diminish the brilliance that emanated from the *linga*, Lord Krishna instructed the Pandavas to bring sand from Ramesvaram to cover it. They removed the *linga* from the *kund* and installed it as Nageshwara *jyotirlinga*.

In this *linga* dwells both Vishnu and Shiva, so it is also called Hari/Hareshwar. This temple's main door is to the west, unlike other temples. This is because the devotee Namdev was in the eastern doorway and the priest asked him to move. So he went to the back of the temple on the west side and worshiped there. Then Hari/Hareshwar turned and faced west to accept his devotee's worship.

BADRINATH

Regarding the holy place of Badrinath in the Himalayas, it is said that Narada Muni and the demigods come to the Badrinatha temple here during the winter months to continue the worship of Badrinath, the Deity of BadriNarayana when the other priests leave for the winter and go to Joshimath. In the middle of November the priests perform one last *puja*, leave the ghee lamps lit, and close the temple. Badrinath stays closed 6 months a year from Deepavali all the way until the full moon day in the month of Chittirai (late spring in the Himalayas). Then in May they return, open the temple, and the ghee lamps are still burning, thanks to the demigods.

The tradition of this temple is explained as follows: Since the history of this temple is so old, the only way we can understand how it came to be is by the explanations in the *Puranas*. In Satya-yuga, the Lord lived at Badarikashrama (Badrinatha) in a visible form. In Treta-yuga, the sages saw the Lord through the practice of yoga. Then during the age of Dvapara-yuga, it became difficult even for the sages to see the Lord. So then the sages and even the demigods prayed to the Lord, "You are our only supporter, please do not leave this place and ourselves."

Being pleased by their devotion, the Supreme said, "My dear ones and saints! After some time Kali-yuga will start. People in that age will be full of sins, wickedness, pride, and without any pious action. So I cannot stay in a visible form before them. But here under Narada Shila in the Alakananda [River], there is a divine image of mine, which you may take and establish. If one sees that image, he will get the same reward of seeing me in visible form."

After that, Brahma and the other gods took that image out of the Narada Kund in the river and asked Visvakarma, the architect of the gods, to build a temple, after which they established the Deity there. Narada Muni was made their official priest, and a rule was made that the Deity would be worshiped for six months by human beings, and the other six months by the gods. And this rule is still followed to this day.

In the *Skanda Purana* another story is told relating how the Deity of Badrivishal was established. Therein it is explained that Lord Shankar (Shiva) told his son Skanda that in Kali-yuga, in his incarnation as a saint (Shankaracharya), he would take the Deity from Narada Kund and install it. Thus, by seeing that Deity, all the sins of a person will be removed in a moment, just as the heard of elephants run away by seeing a lion. So after some time, Lord Shankara took birth as Shankaracharya and established the Deity of Sri Badrinathji for the general good of all people.

How this happened is further related. At the tender age of twelve, Shankaracharya went to Badarikashrama after a hard three months of travel up into the mountains with his pupils. He took bath in the hot springs of Taptakund and went into the temple, but the four-armed form of Narayana that had been established by the rishis in Satya-yuga was not there. In its place was a *shalagram-shila* stone, which is considered the same as the Lord. But Shankaracharya went outside the temple with a heavy heart, followed by the temple priests. He asked them, "Why is the temple without Narayana's form? I have heard that the Lord resides here in this pious place for the last four *yugas.*"

The priests replied, "Because of the tyranny of Chinese robbers, our ancestors hid that form of the Lord in the nearby *kund.* But after that it was difficult to find. So from that time on we have allowed the *shalagram-shila* to reside on the altar." So Shankaracharya asked them if the form of the Lord could be found, would they install and worship it in the temple. The priests all agreed.

Then Shankaracharya went to the *kund* and meditated, and then went into the water. The priests asked him not to go since there was a current below in which many people had lost their lives. But Shankaracharya did not listen. He went deep into the *kund* and pulled out a Deity of Lord Narayana to everyone's astonishment. But the fingers on the right hand of the Deity were broken, so he went back in and pulled out another Deity, but the same fingers were broken. Then he did that a third time and became perplexed until a voice told him, "Shankara, you need not be confused. In this Kali-yuga, only this broken form will be worshiped." So in this way, Shankaracharya came out of the water with the lost Deity and installed it in the temple in a solemn manner. He established one of his disciples, Nambudri Brahmana, for doing the worship. In this way, the Deity and the temple were again established by Sri Shankaracharya. Today, people of all races, creeds, religions, and communities go there with respect to see the Deity of Lord Narayana, Badrivishal.

This story shows the antiquity of the temple and of Deity worship itself, and how Shankaracharaya, in his most inner sentiments, did not follow his teachings of impersonalism but was instead a great devotee of Lord Vishnu or Krishna and also advised the process of Deity worship for the benefit of everyone.

TIRUPATI

There are many, many stories about the Deity of Lord Vishnu at the hilltop temple at Tirupati, and how people offer this Deity their prayers or donations for their wishes to come true, whatever they may be. Unfortunately, many such prayers are for varieties of material facility, but He listens to them all. I knew one friend who climbed the hills and was determined not to ask the Deity for anything, only pure devotional service. But as he was climbing the stairs, he had a severe tooth ache. He could not help but keep thinking about the pain and wishing it would go away. Then when he reached the top and went to see the Deity, he noticed that his toothache had completely gone. No pain at all. He felt that though he did not ask for it intentionally, the Deity still heard his thoughts and removed his pain.

The powerful and very opulent Deity of Lord Vishnu at Tirupati,
also known as Sri Venkateshvara or more simply as Sri Balaji.

CHAPTER SIX

Stories of Lord Jagannatha in Puri

The temple of Lord Jagannatha in Jagannatha Puri is a most important place for the devotees of Lord Krishna and pilgrims who long to visit this place. It is known that Lord Jagannatha is a most lively Deity, showing Himself to many devotees in many ways. So we give a special chapter to relate a few stories just on Lord Jagannatha.

The significance of Jagannatha Puri and the story of how the Deities first appeared goes back many hundreds of years to the time of King Indradyumna, who was a great devotee of Lord Vishnu. One time in his court the King heard from another devotee about an incarnation of Lord Vishnu, named Nila-madhava. (Nila-madhava is the Deity form of Lord Vishnu.) The King very much wanted to see this form of the Supreme and sent many brahmanas to search for Nila-madhava. All came back unsuccessful except for Vidyapati, who did not come back at all. He had wandered to a distant town which was populated by a tribe of people known as Shabaras of non-Aryan heritage. He had stayed in the house of Visvasu, and later, at Visvasu's request, married his daughter, Lalita.

After some time Vidyapati noticed that Visvasu would leave the house every night and return at noon the next day. Vidyapati asked his wife about this. Though her father had ordered her not to tell anyone, she told Vidyapati that Visvasu would go in secret to worship Nila-madhava. After repeated requests, Vidyapati finally got permission to go see Nila-madhava, only if he went blindfolded. But Vidyapati's wife had bound some mustard seeds in his cloth so that a trail could be left to follow later. When they reached the shrine, Vidyapati saw the Deity Nila-madhava after the Shabara took off the

104

blindfold, and he felt great ecstasy.

The story continues to relate that while Visvasu was out collecting items for worship, Vidyapati saw a bird fall into the nearby lake and drown. The soul of the bird suddenly took a spiritual form and ascended back to the spiritual world. Vidyapati wanted to do the same and climbed the tree to jump in the lake. Then a voice from the sky declared that before he jumped he should tell Indradyumna that he had found Nila-madhava.

When Visvasu returned to worship the Deity, Nila-madhava spoke and said that He had accepted the simple worship from him for so many days, but now He wanted to accept the opulent worship that would be offered by King Indradyumna. When Vidyapati went back to tell the King, Indradyumna immediately went to find Nila-madhava but could not locate Him. So the King arrested Visvasu, but a voice told him to release the Shabara and that he should build a temple on top of Nila Hill where the King would see the Lord as Daru-brahman, the wooden manifestation of the Absolute.

After great endeavor, King Indradyumna built the temple at Sri Kshetra, now known as Jagannatha Puri, and later prayed to Lord Brahma to consecrate it. However, Lord Brahma said that it was not within his power to consecrate the temple since Sri Kshetra is manifested by the Supreme's own internal potency and is where the Lord manifests Himself. So Brahma simply put a flag on top of the temple and blessed it, saying that anyone who from a distance saw the flag and offered obeisances would easily be liberated from the material world. So now, anyone who merely sees the flag on top of the present temple and in the mood of devotion offers obeisances to it can be freed from material existence. Nonetheless, after much waiting the King had become anxious since Nila-madhava had not manifested Himself. Thinking his life was useless, the King decided he should end his life by fasting. But in a dream the Lord said that He would appear floating in from the sea in His form as Daru-brahman.

The King went to the shore and found a huge piece of wood that had the markings of a conch, disc, club, and lotus. This was Daru-brahman. But try as they might, the men could not budge the wood. In a dream the Lord spoke to the King and instructed him to get Visvasu and put a golden chariot in front of Daru-brahman. After doing this and forming a *kirtana* party to chant the holy names, and praying for Daru-brahman to mount the chariot, Daru-brahman was easily moved. Lord Brahma then performed a sacrifice where the present temple now stands and installed a Deity of Lord Narasimhadeva, the half-man and half-lion Deity that is now on the western side of the temple.

From the wooden Daru-brahman, the King requested many expert carvers to carve the form of the Deity, but none could do so for their chisels immediately broke when they touched the wood. Finally, the architect of the demigods, Visvakarma, (some say the Lord Himself) arrived as an old artist, Ananta Maharana, and promised that he would carve the Deity form of the Lord inside the temple in three weeks if the King would allow him to work behind closed doors. But after 14 days the King became very anxious because he could no longer hear the sounds of the carving. Finally, he could stand it no more. On the advice of the queen, he personally opened the doors of the temple to see what was happening. Then he saw the forms of Lord Jagannatha, Lord Balarama, and Lady Subhadra. But because the King had opened the doors sooner than he was supposed to, the Deities were not completed: Their feet and hands had not yet been carved. Thus, the Supreme manifested Himself in this form.

The King felt he had committed a great offense for having opened the doors before the allotted three weeks had passed, so he decided to end his life. But in a dream Lord Jagannatha told the King that though he had broken his promise, this was just a part of the Supreme's pastimes to display this particular form. Occasionally, the King could decorate the Deity with golden hands and feet. Yet, those devotees who were filled with love would always see the form of Lord Jagannatha as the threefold bending form of Syamasundara, Krishna, holding a flute. Thus, the Supreme appeared in this form so that people could approach and see Him, especially as He rides on the huge carts during the Ratha-Yatra festival.

Lord Jagannath as He is seen on the last night of the great Ratha festival as He stands on the Ratha Yatra cart wearing His Suna Vesha outfit and with golden ornaments and hands that hold His golden chakra and conch shell.

This next story and the following two are from "The Lilas of Lord Jagannatha" by Mr. Somanath Khuntia, a writer and priest who serves in the temple. His book contains many stories of actual miracles that have happened in the temple, or to devotees connected with Lord Jagannatha. These are but a few.

LORD JAGANNATHA AND DASIA BOURI

It is useless to ask whether Dasia Bouri was of sound mind to offer a coconut to the Deity of the Lord, and then ask, "Please return it to me if the Lord does not accept it happily." This was certainly strange. Is there such a God who can take offerings in His own hands from devotees?

Anyone who goes to the temple offers such things as coconuts, mangos, bananas, and other items, but it is accepted that they are sanctified through many rituals before the offering is made, which makes them eligible for being accepted by the Deity. So how is it that a coconut was offered to the Lord Himself as if He were in dire need of it? So Dasia Bouri instructed the priest, "Let it be offered as it is. Otherwise, it is to be returned."

The chief priest of Dasia Bouri's village entered the temple a second time with the coconut in his hand. Already he had *darshan* of the Lord, and all the *bhoga* or unoffered food had been offered to the Deity. However, the priest had forgotten the coconut. Just for the sake of formality, he was going to show the coconut before the Deity of the Lord to fulfill Dasia Bouri's request and then return it to him.

Inside the inner sanctum of the temple, there was a big rush. Near the Garuda-stambha was a little free space. So the priest moved there to have a clear view. He prayed, "Oh Lord, accept this offering from Dasia Bouri from the nearby village of Baligram. He is of a caste that is excluded from the temple. But he has requested that if You don't accept it in Your own hands, then it must be returned unoffered."

While people were crowding around the priest, he held up the coconut before Lord Jagannatha. He felt as if his hands were frozen around it. Suddenly, the coconut began slipping out of his grasp!

Then it disappeared miraculously! The priest and everyone else were awestruck by this miracle.

The priest wondered, "Dasia Bouri is a devotee of colored caste, an untouchable. How was it possible in this age of Kali-yuga for the Lord to take such a man's offering in His own hands?"

Suddenly, another priest near Lord Jagannatha's altar shouted, "Oh, what a catastrophe! Pieces of coconut shell are falling all around here!"

The details of this incident quickly became known by all. Everyone wondered about it, and thought it was a trick. But this mattered little to the Lord and His devotee. "You cannot realize God except through faith," Dasia Bouri's father had told him.

Dasia belonged to the nearby village of Baligram, which exists even today some 30 miles from Puri. Life in the village goes on much as it did then in the 1790s. Dasia had a wife but no children. He was a weaver by occupation. Usually, he sang hymns to the Lord in the evening in his simple hut. Singing was spontaneous to him and new songs to Jagannatha were always pouring from his lips, even though he could not read or write. He felt the reverberations from these songs throughout his body. He often felt as if he were being embraced by God and once heard the utterance, "I have created everybody. All are My sons and daughters. There is no untouchability and no separation between Me and anyone."

The time of the Rathayatra or Chariot Festival was nearing. Jagannatha would come outside so that people of all castes and religions could see Him. Eagerly that morning Dasia Bouri also set out on foot for Puri, 30 miles away. He sang sweetly all the way, charming his fellow pilgrims with his devotional songs. When the group arrived, it was already time for the pulling of the chariots to begin. So he waited near Balagandi Street, halfway down the Grand Road of Puri, instead of going nearer to the temple. It is the fervent belief of devotees that one can be purged of all sins at the slightest touch of the ropes used in pulling the chariots. Dasia Bouri felt as if he were being pulled toward the chariot of Lord Balabhadra, instead of himself pulling it. Then as if in a vision, he saw Subhadra's chariot approaching. To his God-intoxicated mind, Subhadra's chariot appeared to be running ahead.

Decorated in gorgeous colors, the chariot of Lord Jagannatha followed last, to the resounding thunder of clanging cymbals and blowing conch shells. The chariot was headed by four white wooden stallions and was being pulled vigorously by tens of thousands of devotees.

"What a gracious countenance! What large, loving eyes! Oh, such a face! It is like the dark sky itself! How inviting His smile, reaching out His big arms to embrace us all!" Dasia Bouri thought to himself. He wished to go up to the chariot, but his wish could never be fulfilled, for he was an untouchable. "Is it an offense to touch Jagannatha, who is Lord of the entire cosmos?" Dasia's only consolation was that he was seeing Jagannatha before him on the best of days and in the Lord's best mood. To be near His divine presence was all Dasia could think of.

The Lord's image fully held Dasia Bouri's attention. He was overwhelmed with feelings of intense love and devotion. In such a state, Dasia Bouri walked back to his village, with the Lord's songs on his lips and the Lord's image imprinted on his heart.

His wife was waiting for him. She had prepared simple rice water for his meal. In the middle of the bowl of white rice, one dark leaf of spinach was floating. In his highly elated state, Dasia saw it as one of the big round eyes of Jagannatha.

The entire atmosphere of the home was saturated with the Lord's divine presence. Seeing her husband dancing, the wife thought he must have become possessed by some ghost.

"The food resembles my Lord! How can I eat it?" was all Dasia could reply.

Then Lord Jagannatha appeared to Dasia Bouri and spoke, "Oh, Dasia! I am always with you. I have no need for a diamond pedestal. Ask whatever you like. I am prepared to bless you!"

At bedtime, Dasia Bouri whispered to Lord Jagannatha, "Oh, Lord. I only ask this. Please accept my offerings of Your own accord, whenever I offer You anything." The Lord gave a nod of agreement and disappeared.

The next morning Dasia Bouri procured a coconut from his landlord, bartering a piece of cloth for it. The coconut must be offered to the Lord, only then could his dream be verified. But how could the coconut be sent to Jagannatha? By the Lord's arrangement, the head priest of his village happened to be going that very day to Puri with a group of devotees bearing many offerings. Dasia humbly approached the brahmana priest, asking, "O friend, please take this to Lord Jagannatha on my behalf, as I am unable to go inside the temple. If He does not take it, please return it to me when you come back."

After the illuminating incident in the temple, all realized, including the village priest himself, that the Lord and His devotee are inseparable. "Where there is a pure devotee, I Myself am present."

Once Dasia Bouri went to Puri on his own with a basket of mangos for the Lord. On arriving in Puri, he envisioned the image of Jagannatha sitting inside the blue wheel on top of the temple, called Nila-chakra. Jagannatha accepted the fruit of his own accord, and the basket was immediately emptied. A group of temple priests saw this miraculous disappearance of the mangos and rushed to Jagannatha to ascertain the genuineness of the incident. To their utter amazement, they found mango skins and pits lying on the altar, and drops of mango juice running down the face of Jagannatha!

Who will label such a devotee as "low" or "untouchable." There was such complete union between this devotee and Lord Jagannatha, like a lover and his beloved! Is not such a person blessed?!

After the death of Dasia Bouri, the King of Puri granted his descendants a role in the annual Chariot Festival. They alone would be allowed to carry the wooden horses and the three charioteers to the chariots. This service is performed to this day only by members of his family.

LORD JAGANNATHA AND BANDHU MOHANTI

Bandhu Mohanti was a non-brahmana, but he was a great devotee of Lord Jagannatha. As poor as he was, he believed that Lord Jagannatha was his true friend and would come to help him in his hour of need.

Bandhu Mohanti used to spend most of the day only reading about Lord Jagannatha, forgetting his wife and children. His wife did not even know that her husband was a devotee of Lord Jagannatha. She only thought that he has some local friend known by the name of Jagannatha. She was much annoyed when Bandhu Mohanti wanted to spend more time with his friend than with her. One day the wife asked, "Who is that friend?"

Bandhu Mohanti replied, "You do not know and you cannot know. He is very rich, having a great building. He is a king and His dress, His behavior, His life style, everything about Him is royal. He is also very kind."

"Let us go see him some time!" the wife requested.

"How can you go in such a poor dress?" the husband answered. "If we want to go, we must take with us some gifts, and our children must wear good clothes. You must wear a gold necklace and bangles, otherwise the gatekeeper of my friend's house may not allow us to enter. Since I have no money to buy such things, I am not going to meet Him," he added. Bandhu Mohanti's wife replied, "If your friend is true and faithful, he will respect you and accept you in whatever dress you wear. Since you are so poverty stricken, why don't you approach him for help?"

Bandhu Mohanti paid no attention to what his wife said, and so his wife became very angry again. Even more difficult times were coming. The whole village was suffering from a bad harvest, as no rain had come, many might die of starvation. It was the year 1392, and like Bandhu Mohanti, most of the villagers were farmers. All were greatly worried. Bandhu Mohanti was often telling them, "My friend is rich. If He wishes, we can be saved." So his wife forcibly made Bandhu Mohanti go and meet this great friend.

It was after dark when Bandhu Mohanti, accompanied by his wife and three children, started out for Puri to meet Lord Jagannatha. The wife was thinking, "If we come to any town, at least someone will give the children some food." So they came walking from the village Shatapada to Puri, nearly 30 miles away. Only a few grains of rice were shared with them by the pilgrims who passed them on the road that night.

After three days, they finally reached Puri. Bandhu Mohanti took them straight to the temple of Lord Jagannatha, but as it was the middle of the night, the doors were closed. So they rested at Pejanala on the southern side of the temple. This is the outside watering trough where cows come to drink the rice water drained from the temple kitchen.

"Where is he, your rich friend here at Puri? Where is his house? When are we going there?" asked his wife anxiously.

"He is very nearby now," Bandhu Mohanti replied. He did not wish to tell her that he meant Lord Jagannatha was his friend. The children were hungry and crying. So the wife gave them rice water to drink from Pejanala, where the cows come to drink. Afterwards they went to sleep. Bandhu Mohanti also slept. But as his wife was feeling so worried for the children, she woke up. Suddenly she saw a young dark brahmana carrying many different types of food over his head on a golden tray. He came near, shouting, "Where is Bandhu Mohanti? Where is Bandhu Mohanti?" The wife heard this, as he was shouting in a loud voice. "Yes, we are here. What is the matter?" she asked.

The young brahmana smiled mysteriously and said, "The friend of Bandhu Mohanti has sent him this food. Please take it as I have a lot of other work to do." The wife was not in position to know what to do. Bandhu Mohanti was fast asleep. She did not think it proper to disturb his sleep after such a long journey. The young brahmana was about to leave, so she had no time to ask anything. She accepted all the food on the golden plate and woke her children. They all ate this huge feast, then fell asleep again, their stomach fully satisfied.

When Bandhu Mohanti awoke, he was told everything. He began to cry profusely, "Why didn't you wake me up? You are blessed to see Him. I am unfit to ever meet Him!" His mind was reeling from the magnitude of what had just happened to them. The wife did not understand what the matter was. As she was more worldly-minded, she could not grasp the deep meaning of the incident.

Bandhu Mohanti, in great ecstasy, ate from the golden tray all that was left by the children. "But what should I do with the gold plate?" he asked himself. He cleaned it and with deep devotion he placed it under his pillow that night, lest it be stolen.

In the morning, there was much commotion inside the temple. The costly golden tray used by Lord Jagannatha was missing. The matter was immediately reported to Virakishora, the King of Puri, who is considered to be the "moving Jagannatha" and sole authority on matters of the Jagannatha Temple.

The police caught Bandhu Mohanti as he slept that morning outside the temple walls. The golden tray was returned to the temple, and the King was about to deliver harsh punishment. Bandhu Mohanti's wife and children cried and pleaded. "It was all the doing of Bandhu Mohanti's rich friend!" the wife said, trying to defend her husband. Bandhu Mohanti could not help but cry also. Never did he expect that such a calamity would happen to them. The King announced that he would give the sentence the next day.

That night the King of Puri had a miraculous dream. Lord Jagannatha Himself appeared in the dream, saying, "Oh, King, if a friend come to your house, is it not right that you greet him with a fine meal? Bandhu Mohanti is My friend, so what fault have I done to give him food on My golden tray? Will you sentence Me also? Please, release him at once."

The King was astonished to see Lord Jagannatha come in his dream and tell him all this. He released Bandhu Mohanti forthwith. He also ordered that Bhandhu Mohanti and also his descendants be allowed to serve in the temple itself.

Even now in the temple, descendants of Bandhu Mohanti cook the first meal of the day for Lord Jagannatha. It is a preparation of sweet rice and ghee, known as khecheda. After cooking this *prasada*, Bandhu Mohanti himself was given the privilege of carrying this offering on that very golden tray to the Deities. After the food was offered, he would lead the procession of *maha-prasada* being taken to the devotees, carrying the golden try over his head. Even today there are cooks in the temple with the surname of Mohanti who are direct descendants of Bandhu Mohanti, still carrying out this service.

What is surprising is that Bandhu Mohanti was a non-brahmana and never held any hereditary service in the temple before. Of the more than 15,000 worshipers of the Jagannatha temple today, this can only be said of him. He had simply considered Lord Jagannatha to be his friend.

A WISH FULFILLED

On the first day of a young man's service in the temple of Lord Jagannatha, another miraculous *lila* or pastime occurred. When he was standing before the Deities in the evening, a newly married couple who cam from the state of Bengal met him. The man's name was Deepen Ghosh and the wife's name was Shubhashree.

The husband asked the priest who later retold this event, "Is the one with the black face Jagannatha? Can He really hear prayers and answer them? Perhaps not, because He is made of wood and has no ears to hear with. You, being the priests of Jagannatha, only cheat the innocent pilgrims who come from distant places. You are only interested in taking money from them in His name. But He never answers any of our prayers."

As this was only his first day in the temple, the young *khuntia* or servant could not understand what Mr. Ghosh meant. He simply replied with much feeling, "Yes, Jagannatha does hear, if your prayer is sincere."

Deepen Ghosh was a wealthy businessman and he was very skeptical of these ancient traditions. So he sarcastically rebuffed the young man, "I am sincere, but you are not. What is the use of doing *puja* and prayer to that log of wood? The father has told the son to do this, and the son has told his son. Like that, it goes on and on. The one whom you call Jagannatha can never hear you."

When the man became more adamant to challenge Jagannatha, the young priest consulted with the head priest, who was decorating Lord Jagannatha with flower garlands at that time. The head priest advised, "Tell him to come again for the Chandana Lagi ceremony of Jagannatha after midnight. At that time, Jagannatha's forehead is smeared with sweet-smelling sandal before He retires to bed. If any person prays to Him at this particular hour, He grants the prayer."

When Mr. Ghosh again began to abuse Lord Jagannatha with sarcastic remarks and loud laughter, his young wife bowed her head in prayer. When he left the temple, she silently followed. To the amazement of all, this same Mr. Ghosh and his wife turned up for the

Chandana Lagi ceremony that very night. He met the young priest there and put the same question again, "So, is this a good time for Jagannatha to listen? If so, I have something to ask Him."

The young priest inquired as to what he wanted. Mr Ghosh retorted, "Can He give it to me? You ask Him first!" The priest, being disgusted with this difficult man, told him, "Yes, He will grant it to you, just tell Him what you want."

Mr. Ghosh looked a moment at his beautiful young wife. Her skin was light and her face shone like that of a goddess. She was wearing a rich Benares silk saree and her face was half-covered with its cloth. Then, half in joke and half in deep sincerity, he turned to Lord Jagannatha and asked, "Tell Him to give me salvation. Tell Him I am asking for His *moksha*."

The young *khuntia* went to the head priest, who was putting sandalwood paste on Lord Jagannatha's forehead at that moment. It is but natural that at such an enjoyable moment Lord Jagannatha would be in a good mood and happy to grant anything asked for. The *khuntia* communicated all the details about the man to the head priest. His name, his native place, his wife's name, and the prayer itself.

Then in a big voice so that the man himself could hear, the priest asked Lord Jagannatha, "Oh, Jagannatha, this man Deepen Ghosh from Bengal asks that You grant him liberation. Please grant this."

The young priests returned and told the man that his prayer would be granted.

Mr. Ghosh replied, "Hah! This wooden Deity! It granted my prayer! Wonderful! Don't cheat me, please. Don't cheat me. Don't think I am so stupid, I can't be fooled so easily."

Months passed. This incident slipped from the young priest's mind. Some six months later, he was returning home from his work at school. As he passed by the main East Gate of the temple, he heard his name announced over the temple loudspeakers. "Sri Somanatha Khuntia, please come to the information counter because a lady from Bengal has come to meet you."

The *khuntia* was very surprised. "What lady wants to meet me?" He went quickly to the information counter. On seeing the lady, he could not recollect ever meeting her before. She was wearing a plain white sari, without any makeup or gold ornament. She was a widow in mourning. More than this, he could not gather.

Seeing the young priest coming, the lady rushed to him and fell at his feet out of respect for a priest of the temple. She also put 101 rupees at his feet. In tears, she said, "Actually, your Jagannatha is very great. He hears just like a man, and now I am a widow, as my young husband, Deepen Ghosh, died suddenly only last month." The young priest then remembered everything and stood speechless. This is the miraculous power and personality of the Deity who is indeed able to see and hear everything, and do anything when He wants.

CHAPTER SEVEN

More Recent Personal Experiences

      This chapter contains a few of the more recent and personal stories that I have heard from people who have had their own experiences with Deities of the Supreme, or His various incarnations and forms.

      Sometimes devotees are humble and are hesitant to share what are intimate experiences with the Deities due to fear of them being misunderstood. And some will share but will prefer that they remain anonymous out of either humility, or that others will view them as being unqualified for such events in their lives. But the interactions with Deities happen to many people on a regular basis, for many reasons. Sometimes their health is in grave or serious condition, which is then alleviated after doing serious prayers to the Deities. Or sometimes couples who have not been able to have children pray sincerely to the Deities and later find that they are expecting a child.

      Even with the Deities at the nearby Krishna temple here in Detroit, called Devasadan Mandir, I have seen where people have had difficulties with their immigration status and have but a week or two before they must leave America. Then I have instructed them to drop their ego and open their hearts and go in front of the Deities that we have here of Sri Sri Radha-Kunjabihari and express their fear and concerns, and ask for help. Another week or so later they came back to let me know that their immigration status had been resolved. Or in another case, a couple was trying to have children, but nothing had yet developed. Later, after praying to the Deities, they had a healthy baby. I have also seen where practically impossible projects had

*The lovely and most merciful Deities of Sri Sri Radha-Kunjabihari
at the Krishna temple in Detroit, Michigan*

been proposed to the Deities, such as making a new hall, or different developments around the building, and so on, and when the devotees wished and prayed devotedly enough, difficult things came together very quickly by the blessings of the Deities.

These kinds of things have happened all over the world, but I have seen this happen several times here in Detroit in relation to our Sri Sri Radha-Krishna Deities, or with our Deities of Lord Jagannatha, Balarama and Subhadra. These Deities have done miracles for Their devotees in the past and continue to do so. All it takes is to go before the Deities and open up to the blessings They can provide. But first you must humble yourself and then reveal your hearts with faith, and then with trust be open for whatever may happen, and miracles can and have taken place. This is especially beneficial and shows that the Deities are real. This also increases the faith and devotion of the persons who experience or witness this. But extra merit is earned when a person simply prays for continued devotional service to the Deity and deeper levels of love for God.

LADDU GOPAL AT SRI KHANDA

This is from a lecture by H.H. Jayapataka Swami, a story that has been told many times.

There is a Deity of Gopal Krishna, a small Gopal, "laddu Gopal" we call Him. This is in Sri Khanda. There lives Mukundananda and his wife, and their son was Raghunanda. The father had to go and see some disciple who was on his death bed. So he quickly gave the initiation to his son with the *ugranaya*, first mantra of the Gayatri mantra, and instructed, "You can worship the Deity. Your mother will tell you what to do. I have to go to see my disciple, to help him remember Krishna at the time of death." The he went off.

The mother said, "You just go in, you ask the Deity to accept the laddus, then you come back with the plate."

So he went to the Deities, put the laddus there, and asked the Deity to accept: "Please accept these laddus." But it seemed that the Deity wasn't accepting them. He didn't see, so he cried, "hhuhh huhhh."

The Deity asked, "Why are you crying?"

"You are not taking the laddus."

"You want me to eat?"

"Oh, yes. My mother said you would eat."

Then the Deity became a little boy and started eating the laddus. The boy came back with an empty plate to his mother.

The mother looked at the empty plate. "Where are the laddus?"

"Oh, the Deity ate them," said the boy. She was wondering what's happening? This was going on every day, and the Deity was taking every day.

When Mukundananda came back, the mother told him this is happening. He said, "I'll hide in the temple and watch what is happening." Then he came behind the Deity, and was listening. He heard the boy say, "Please accept these laddus. Eat them." Then he didn't hear anything. He looked up, and he saw the Deity eating the laddus. The Deity had become like a little boy and was eating the laddus.

"Huh!" he gasped. After all, in most cases you don't expect to see the Deity eating laddus like that. He was shocked. When He heard the gasp, the Deity became stone again. But in his hand He had a half-eaten laddu.

Since then they offer the Deity half a laddu.

So the boy became very famous. The Deity was eating from his hand.

When Raghunanda grew up, he established the Lord Chaitanya dancing Deity in Khatwa, at the place where Lord Chaitanya took sannyasa.

GOPAL GIRI

Gadai Giri had only one son, who was named Gopal Giri. Gopal Giri was influenced by the devotional qualities of his father and was very devoted to Lord Jagannath. Every year he would go to Puri to see the Ratha-Yatra festival. He was also very attached to performing *sankirtan*, and was expert in many different styles of *kirtan*.

Gopal Giri had a desire to worship a Deity of Gopal. Unable to find such a Deity, he decided to go to Puri, thinking that if he would render service to Lord Jagannath there, then somehow Gopal would come to him. Arriving in Puri, he stayed in the area known as Kundei Benta Sahi, near Grand Road. As he was very scholarly, he easily obtained service in the office of the king, where he became the poddar, or cashier, for the Temple of Lord Jagannath.

Gopal Giri led a very regulated life. While staying in Puri he would daily go to see Lord Jagannath, and at the temple he would sit on the *bais pahaca*, the twenty-two steps inside the compound leading up to the main *darshan* area, and there he would read *Srimad-Bhagavatam*. In the evening he would take *prasad* and go home. Every Sunday he would go to the Satalahari Math, a temple near the ocean, where he would sit and read *Srimad-Bhagavatam* and chant *harinam*, the Lord's holy names. He was very attached to *Srimad-Bhagavatam*.

During the Ratha-Yatra festivals in Puri, he would approach

devotees and *sadhus* coming from Vrindavana and ask them to bring him back a Deity of Gopal. They would readily agree. "Yes, yes," they would say. "Next time I will bring a Gopal Deity for you." But no one ever brought a Deity. At this same time, in Vrindavana there was one renounced devotee who was worshiping a Deity of Gopal. One night this Gopal Deity appeared in the sannyasi's dream and spoke to him.

In this regard, Sri Srimad Gour Govinda Swami tells this story:

"Gopal Giri was serving in Puri as a government cashier. He was always thinking in his mind, 'If I can get a Gopal Deity, I'll offer worship to Him.' But he thought, 'How can I go to Vrindavan?' He had a strong desire to get a Deity.

"At that time this Deity of Gopal was in Vrindavan with a sannyasi Vaishnava, a renunciant. He was doing *madhukari*, begging, and he was keeping that Deity in his *jhola* (a cloth tied as a bag). During the day, he would go out and do *madhukari*, then in the evening he would cook whatever he had begged and offer it to Gopal. In this way, he was leading his life.

"One night this Gopal Deity told the Vaisnava, 'You take me to Gopal Giri, the son of Gadai Giri. He wants to offer Me worship. I want to go there. Take me there.'

"But the Vaishnava sannyasi thought that it was only a dream. He did not take it seriously. After a few days Gopal came again in a dream and beat him with a cane on his legs. It was such a severe beating that his legs were bleeding. The sannyasi Vaishnava woke up and begged, apologizing, 'Please forgive me for my offense. I did not take Your order seriously. But You have beaten me so severely, how can I go there with such wounds on my legs?'

"Gopal said, 'When Gopal Giri touches you, it will be healed, otherwise you cannot be cured. You go there at once. Don't make any delay.'

"So he started walking. At that time there was no communication system, no train or bus. The only way was by walking. It took him two and a half months to reach Puri. At this time Gopal Giri was staying in a rented house at Kundhei Benta Sahi in Puri. The Vaishnava reached Puri in the evening and stayed near the

Jagannath temple. Early the next morning he inquired, 'Who is Gopal Giri? I want to meet him.'

"Many people knew Gopal Giri. He was famous as the cashier of the Jagannath temple. So he quickly found Gopal Giri at his rented house.

"Gopal Giri had just finished his bath and was putting on *tilak*. The Vaisnava arrived and offered his obeisances to Gopal Giri. He then took the Deity from his bag and presented Him to Gopal Giri. Gopal Giri was amazed. 'What is this? Who are you, and where has this Deity come from?'

"The Vaisnava replied, 'You wanted Gopal to worship, so Gopal has come from Vrindavana. I was in Vrindavana carrying this Gopal. He told me to hand Him over to you, and He beat me when I did not listen.' He showed Gopal Giri his legs and said, 'If you touch it, it will be cured; otherwise it will not be cured.' So Gopal Giri immediately touched him and the injury was gone.

"Gopal Giri was very happy that Gopal had fulfilled his desire. He couldn't go to Vrindavana, but Gopal had come to him. Gopal Giri went to the market and purchased rice, dal, and vegetables. He prepared *prasad* and gave some to the Vaishnava. Then he went to the king and offered his resignation, saying, 'I don't want to serve any more.'

"When he returned to his room he opened his bag and told that Vaishnava, 'You can take as much money as you want.' The Vaishnava said, 'No, I don't want any money. I only want to do service for Gopal. Wherever Gopal goes, I will go. I want to go and serve Him. I am not one to sell Gopal. I am a servant. I won't take any money.'

"Later on, Gopal Giri again went to see the king. The king asked him, 'Why did you resign?' 'I have a Temple in my village and I had a desire to get a Deity of Gopal to worship.' The king was very pleased and said, 'All right, your desire is very noble. I have no objection. But sometimes you must come to Puri with your *kirtan* party and chant in Jagannath's temple.'

The king gave Gopal Giri some extra months of salary and allowed him to go. Gopal Giri then sent a message to Gadeigiri for a *kirtan* group to come to Puri to accompany Gopal to His new home.

When the Gajapati king heard the *kirtan* of the Gadeigiri villagers he became very pleased. It is written in the *Mada La-panji*, the history book of the Temple of Lord Jagannath, that whenever the *kirtan* party from Gadeigiri comes they should be allowed to perform *kirtan* in the temple.

Gopal Giri installed the Gopal Deity in Gadeigiri and requested the renunciant from Vrindavana to perform Gopal's daily worship. After serving Gopal for twenty years, the renunciant departed this world and was given *samadhi*, ritual burial, near Gopal's temple. After this, Gopal Giri engaged other renounced Vaishnavas in the daily worship of Gopal.

How Gopal Came to Iskcon

The following story is about how Gopal came to Iskcon, adopted from the book *Gopal Jiu-The Beloved Deity of Srila Gour Govinda Swami* (by Gopal Jiu publications, pages 55 - 61).

Ghanashyam Giri's father, Gopinath Giri, departed this world in 1964. From 1964 until 1992 Ghanashyam Giri was entrusted with serving Gopal. He worked very hard to make Gopal happy, but after some time he found that there was very little help. Concerned about how Gopal's service could be maintained, he remembered his cousin-brother Braja-bandhu Manik who had become a *sannyasi-guru* in Iskcon and was now known as Gour Govinda Swami Maharaja. Ghanashyam Giri thought that since Gour Govinda Swami had so much devotion for Gopal, he would be the appropriate person to whom to pass on the service of Gopal.

In the meantime, Gour Govinda Swami was regularly coming to Gadeigiri for *darshan*. Before and after traveling abroad for his preaching tours he would always seek the blessings of Gopal. In 1989 Gour Govinda Swami began bringing devotees from the large Iskcon Temple in Bhubaneswar to Gadeigiri to celebrate Radhastami, the appearance festival of Srimati Radharani. This developed into a grand festival of *kirtana*, lectures and *prasad* distribution, and many of the local villagers would enthusiastically participate. Again, Ghanashyam Giri decided to give Gopal to Gour Govinda Swami. They discussed the matter and Gour Govinda Swami happily agreed to accept the responsibility. But shortly thereafter Ghanashyam Giri began again to have second thoughts. If he gave Gopal to the guru of so many Westerners, would Gopal then belong to the Western corner? One year went by, and seeing his reluctance Gour Govinda Swami became disappointed.

Ghanashyam Giri describes the incident that changed his mind: About 2:30 one morning I had a dream. Gopal came and was standing near my head. He said, "Why are you sleeping? Wake up! So many troubles have come to you, but have you felt any difficulty? No, because I am always behind you. Now you are alone. How can you arrange all types of festivals for Me? I am always very interested to hear *nama-sankirtana*. Gour Govinda Swami is your own relative. Why don't you give Me to him? So, now tell Me, will you give Me or not?"

In the dream I said, "Yes. Yes. I will give. I will give." Suddenly my wife woke me up and said, "What are you saying? What will you give? To whom will you give? You are speaking like a madman. What happened?" I told her that Gopal had just come and asked me if I was going to give Him to Gour Govinda Swami or not and I said, "Yes. Yes. I will give. I will give." I told her, "Gopal was standing near that window. He just left."

My wife said gently, "Go and donate Gopal to Srila Gurudeva. Whatever property you have you should also give to him. If he takes Gopal, then Gopal will be happy and He will be taken care of nicely. You will be able to see Gopal here every day. Why are you hesitating?" In this way, my doubt was cleared.

The next day I was preparing to go to Bhubaneswar to see Gour Govinda Swami, but I heard that Gurudeva was coming to Gadeigiri. So I stayed and waited for his arrival. He came a few days later and I met with him. He asked me, "How are you? What about Gopal?" I said, "I have been waiting for you to come, to give Gopal to you."

Gurudeva looked at me for a moment and laughed. He said, "What has happened to you? What has brought about this change?" He said, "Has Gopal spoken to you?" I said, "Yes, Gurudeva, Gopal spoke to me." Then Gurudeva asked me, "What day was it that He spoke to you, and what time?" I told him, "Twelve days before, at 2:30 in the morning." Gurudeva nodded his head up and down.

"Gopal came and spoke with me on the same morning at 2:00 am, then at 2:30 He came to you. That morning I was translating the *Bhagavatam* into Oriya. I dozed off for a few moments.

"Gopal came to me and said, 'You installed Radha-Gopinath here. Has Gopinath replaced Me in your life?'" (Srila Gour Govinda Swami had commissioned a sculptor to make Deities of Radha and Krishna to be exactly the same height, width, standing position, etc., as Radha Gopal in Gadeigiri, and installed them on the Iskcon property at Bhubaneswar, naming them Radha-Gopinath).

Gopal again asked Srila Gurudeva, "Is Gopinath the same for you as me?" With folded hands Gurudeva replied, "No." Then Gopal said, "You are worshipping here, but I can't come here. Gadeigiri is the house of My devotees. They have no wealth, but there mind is always on Me. Even if they only offer Me a tulasi leaf and a little water I am happy there. They are always saying, 'Gopal! Gopal!' I cannot leave them and come here. You are not doing any service for Me because Ghanashyam has not given Me to you. He promised, 'Unless Gopal tells me to give Him.'"

Gopal then said, "I will speak to Ghanashyam. First I have met with you and now I am going to Ghanashyam."

While Gurudeva and I were speaking, one of my family members was there. They said, "You are always talking about donating Gopal, but your are only speaking and not giving." I said, "No, today I must donate Gopal to Gurudeva. Bring tulasi and water and chant mantra." Gurudeva asked, "How will you donate to me?" I said, "As *Srimad-Bhagavatam* describes that Bali Maharaja donated to Lord Vamanadev, like that I will donate Gopal to you. You place your hand under mine and I will donate three times with water and tulasi leaf." I called for a brahmana who put tulasi and water in my hand. I said, "First I donate to you Radha Gopal Jiu. Secondly I give you all of Gopal's paraphernalia. Thirdly I donate the property to you. From tomorrow you will take charge."

Gour Govinda Swami immediately accepted Gopal and the property, and on the 15 of November, 1993 he recorded everything in the name of Iskcon, the institution of his spiritual master.

Gour Govinda Swami then sent two of his disciples to Gadeigiri. They arranged to fix the broken temple building and make nice arrangements for Gopal's worship. The existing temple for Gopal was very small and simple. Now that Gopal was under his care, Gour Govinda Maharaja wanted to build something nice for Gopal. He was very eager to see the work begin. On November 23, Fakir Charan went to see Gour Govinda Swami in Bhubaneswar.

Fakir Charan remembers: When he saw us he started scolding us. He said, "The registration was finished eight days ago, where have you been? My dear Gopal's work is not going on correctly. Gopal is beating me." He then showed us his back, which bore fresh marks from a beating. I was shocked. We both begged forgiveness for the delay. He then replied, "The devotee of Krishna never fears anyone. This is service for Krishna, so where is the fear?"

On January 17, 1994 Gour Govinda Swami laid the foundation stone for Gopal's new Temple and he installed a Deity of Anantasesh. On that day, in his lecture he spoke to all of the devotees as well as to the laborers and construction workers who were there to begin work on the new structure that became the new temple for the Deity of Gopal.

THE APPEARANCE OF LORD NARASIMHA
IN MAYAPUR

Here is the story on how the famous Deity of Lord Narasimha manifested at Iskcon Mayapur. This story of how Lord Narasimhadeva came to Sri Mayapur Chandrodaya Mandir is adopted from the Mayapur Journal, based on a discussion with HG Atma Tattva Prabhu.

It all started when on the 24th of March, 1984, at 12.20 a.m., thirty-five dacoits armed with weapons and bombs attacked Sri Mayapur Chandrodaya Mandir. This was an event that many devotees heard about all over the world. They harassed the devotees and treated them with derision. But the greatest shock came when the dacoits decided to steal the Deities of Srila Prabhupada and Srimati Radharani. Fearlessly the devotees challenged the attackers. How could they see Srila Prabhupada and Srimati Radharani carried away? Shots were fired, a few dacoits fell, and their plans foiled. The Deity of Srila Prabhupada was rescued, but the beautiful form of Srimati Radharani would no longer grace the main altar.

This incident really disturbed the minds of the devotees. Those involved in management were especially concerned to make some permanent solution. This was not the first time the devotees had faced violence and harassment in Mayapur. The co-director of Mayapur suggested that Lord Narasimhadeva be installed. When the dacoits had threatened devotees at the Yoga-pitha, Lord Chaitanya's birthplace just down the road, Srila Bhaktivinoda Thakura and his son, Srila Bhaktisiddhanta Sarasvati Thakura, had promptly installed Sri Sri Lakshmi-Narasimhadeva. There had been no further disturbances.

Other devotees in Mayapur were not so keen to follow so closely in these footsteps. The *pujari* of the Deity had to be a *naisthika-brahmachari* (celibate from birth), and the worship of Lord Narasimhadeva must be very strict and regulated. Who would be prepared to worship Him?

Despite such hesitancy, the co-director was enthusiastic to bring Lord Narasimhadeva to Mayapur. He asked Bhaktisiddhanta Dasa and Atma Tattva Prabhu to draw some sketches. One day quite spontaneously he said that the Deity's legs should be bent, ready to jump, he should be looking around ferociously, his fingers should be curled, and flames should be coming from his head. So Atma Tattva Prabhu sketched a Deity in this mood. The devotees liked it, and Pankajanghri Dasa agreed to be the *pujari* and do the worship.

Radhapada Dasa, a wealthy devotee from Calcutta offered to sponsor the sculpting and installation of the Deity. It seemed Lord Narasimhadeva's appearance in Iskcon Mayapur would be a simple, straight-forward affair. Radhapada Dasa promptly gave Rs.1, 30,000 and it was accepted that the Deity would be ready for installation in three months. Atma Tattva Prabhu left for south India to get things organized. By Krishna's grace Atma Tattva soon found a very famous sthapati sculptor. A sthapati not only sculpts Deities, he is also expert in temple architecture and engineering. The man was very obliging until it was mentioned that the Deity to be carved was Ugra-Narasimha, or the form of angry Narasimha. He emphatically refused to make such a Deity. Many Deity sculptors were then approached, but the answer was always the same: No. Atma Tattva Prabhu had made a number of trips between Mayapur and south India, six months had passed, but Lord Narasimhadeva had not yet manifested in His Deity form.

Radhapada Dasa was very anxious to see Lord Narasimhadeva installed in Mayapur. He asked Atma Tattva to visit the original sthapati and once again plead the case. This time the sculptor was a little more congenial and offered to read me a chapter from the *Silpashastra* (a Vedic scripture on sculpture and temple architecture) that deals with the different forms of Deities. He read aloud some verses describing Lord Narasimhadeva. A series of verses described His flame-like mane, his searching glance, and his knees bent with one foot forward ready to jump from the pillar. When he read this, it was exactly the form that was desired.

Atma Tattva Prabhu showed him the sketch he had done. The sculptor was impressed and offered to draw an outline based on the scriptural description which could be used as a guide for sculpting the Deity. He reminded Atma Tattva, though, that he would not carve the form himself.

It took him a week to complete the sketch, and it was very impressive. Atma Tattva Prabhu returned to Mayapur and showed the sketch to the temple authorities. Everyone wanted this same sthapati to carve the Deity. Once again Atma Tattva was sent back to south India to try to convince him. All that could be done was to pray to Lord Narasimhadeva to be merciful and agree to manifest Himself in the temple in Sri Mayapur Dhama.

Atma Tattva had hardly said two sentences when the man very matter-of-factly said he would carve the Deity. The story of how he came to this decision is interesting. The sthapati had approached his guru, the Shankaracharya of Kanchipuram, about the request. His guru's immediate reply was, "Don't do it. Your family will be destroyed." But then, after a moment's reflection, he asked, "Who has asked you to carve this Deity?" When he heard that it was the Hare Krishna people from Navadvipa, he became very concerned. "They want Ugra-Narasimha? Are they aware of the implications of sculpting and installing Ugra-Narasimha? Such Deities were carved over 3,000 years ago by very elevated sthapatis. There is a place on the way to Mysore where a very ferocious Ugra-Narasimha is installed. The demon Hiranyakashipu is torn open on His lap and his intestines are spilling out all over the altar. Once, the standard of worship there was very high. There was an elephant procession and festival everyday. But gradually the worship declined. Today that place is like a ghost town. The whole village is deserted. No one can live there peacefully. Is that what they want for their project?"

The sthapati replied, "They are insistent. They are constantly coming to talk to me about the Deity. Apparently they have some problem with the dacoits."

Handing his guru a sketch of the Deity, he said, "This is the Deity they want." His guru took the sketch and looked at it knowingly. "Ah, this is an Ugra category," he said, "but a Deity in this particular mood is called Sthanu-Narasimha. He doesn't exist on this planet. Even the demigods in the heavenly planets don't worship a form like this. Yes, this Deity belongs to the Ugra category. Ugra means ferocious, very angry. There are nine forms within this category. They are all very fierce. The one they want is Sthanu-Narasimha: stepping out of the pillar. No. Don't carve this Deity. It will not be auspicious for you. I will talk with you about this later."

A few nights later the sthapati had a dream. In the dream his guru came to him and said, "For them you can carve Sthanu-Narasimha." The next morning he received a hand-delivered letter from Kanchipuram. The letter was from the Shankaracharya and gave some instructions regarding temple renovations. There was a footnote at the bottom. It read, "For Iskcon, you can carve Sthanu-Narasimha." The sthapati showed the letter and said, "I have my guru's blessings. I will carve the Deity."

Atma Tattva Prabhu was overwhelmed with joy, and gave him an advance payment and asked him how much time it would take to carve the Deity. He said the Deity would be ready for installation within six months.

Atma Tattva returned to Mayapur. After four peaceful months in the holy *dhama*, it was decided to go to South India and purchase the heavy brass paraphernalia required for the worship of Narasimhadeva and then collect the Deity. The trip was well organized and trouble-free until Atma Tattva visited the sthapati. He explained to the sthapati that all the paraphernalia required for the worship had been purchased and that he had come to collect the Deity. He looked at Atma Tattva as if he'd lost his sense and exclaimed, "What Deity? I have not even found the suitable stone!"

Atma Tattva Prabhu couldn't believe his ears. "But you told me he would be ready in six months," he exclaimed.

"I will keep my promise," the sthapati said. "Six months after I find the stone, the Deity will be ready for installation."

His reply was emphatic, but Atma Tattva just couldn't understand or accept the delay. In frustration he challenged him, "There are big slabs of stone all over South India. What's the problem?"

He looked at Atma Tattva the way a teacher would view a slow student and said very deliberately, "I am not making a grinding mortar, I am making a Deity. The scriptures tell us that only a stone that has life can be used to make a Vishnu Deity. When you hit seven points of the stone slab and they make the sound mentioned in the scriptures, then that stone may be suitable. But there is a second test to indicate whether the stone is a living stone. There is a bug that eats granite. If it eats from one side of the stone to the other and leaves a complete trail visible behind it, then the second test of living stone has been passed. That stone is a living stone, and expression can manifest from it. Only from such a slab can I carve your Narasimhadeva. Such stone speaks poetry. All features of the Deity sculpted from such stone will be fully expressive and beautiful. Please be patient. I've been searching sincerely for your six foot slab."

Atma Tattva Prabhu was amazed and a little anxious. The devotees in Mayapur were expecting the arrival of the Deity soon. How was he going to explain the "living stone" search to them? Maybe they would decide to make Narasimhadeva from marble. Atma Tattva decided to try to lighten the subject by discussing the Prahlada Maharaja *murti* with the sthapati.

"Please forgive me, but I forgot to tell you last time I came that we want a Prahlada *murti*. We want to worship Prahlada-Narasimhadeva. What do you think?"

"I don't think that will be possible," the sthapati replied

matter-of-factly. Atma Tattva looked at him incredulously, not sure
what to say. He smiled and continued, "You want everything done
exactly according to scriptures. Your Narasimhadeva will be four feet
high. Comparatively speaking, that will make Prahlada Maharaja the
size of an amoeba."

"But we want Prahlada Maharaja one foot high."

"Fine," the sthapati replied, "but that means your
Narasimhadeva will have to be about 120 feet high."

We began to argue back and forth about Prahlada Maharaja's
form. Finally, the *sthapati* sighed in resignation and agreed to make
Prahlada Maharaja one foot tall. At least now there was something
positive to report when Atma Tattva returned to Mayapur.

After two months he again returned to South India. There had
been no developments. Atma Tattva Prabhu shuttled back and forth
from Mayapur to South India every thirty or forty days. Finally, the
stone was found and the sthapati became a transformed man. For over
a week he hardly spent any time at home. Hour after hour, day after
day, he just sat staring at the slab. He had a chalk in hand but did not
draw anything. He refused to allow his laborers to do anything except
remove the excess stone to make the slab rectangular. The next time
he was visited, he had made a sketch on the stone. That was all.

The Mayapur managers were becoming impatient. "Are you
sure this Deity will be finished in six months?" Atma Tattva asked
the sthapati in desperation. "Don't worry. The work will be done," he
replied.

After returning to Mayapur, Atma Tattva Prabhu was soon
back in South India to check on some details of the Deity. He found
the sthapati carving the form himself with intense care and
dedication. At that stage the stone had gone and the shape had come.
The sthapati had just started on the armlets. He took two weeks to
carve them. All the features were so refined and delicate. Atma Tattva
was impressed and very happy.

In all, it took the sthapati a little over twelve months to finish
the Deity. When he completed the work he didn't immediately inform
anyone but decided to visit some friends for a few days. It was the
monsoon season, there were few visitors, and he felt it safe to lock up
Lord Narasimhadeva securely in his thatched shed. Two days later his

neighbors ran to inform him that the thatched shed was on fire. There was heavy rain and everything was wet, but the coconut-tree roof had caught fire. He ran to the scene to find Narasimhadeva untouched but the shed burned to ashes.

Immediately he phoned Atma Tattva Prabhu, "Please come and take your Deity. He's burning everything. He's made it clear He wants to go NOW!"

Enthusiastically, Atma Tattva traveled to south India, hired a truck, and half-filled it with sand. He arrived at the sthapati's studio thinking this final stage would be relatively simple. However, he had foolishly forgotten that Lord Narasimhadeva is a very heavy personality: he weighed one ton! After two or three hours they managed to lift the Deity safely from the shed onto the truck. To travel across the border safely, they also needed police permission, along with signed papers from the Central Sales Tax Department, the Archeological Director, and the Art Emporium Department in Tamil Nadu. All the officers demanded to see the Deity before signing the necessary papers. Once they took *darshan* of Lord Narasimhadeva, they all became very obliging and efficient. They had all the necessary papers in hand within twenty-four hours – a miracle given the usual quagmire of bureaucracy found in government offices in India.

The trip back to Mayapur was also amazingly trouble-free and peaceful. Their protector was certainly with them. Usually the sthapati comes on the day of the installation ceremony, goes into the Deity room and carves the eyes of the Deity. This is called *netranimilanam* (opening the eyes). It was an exceptional case that Narasimhadeva's *sthapati* had already carved the eyes. He had not only carved the eyes; he had also done the *prana-pratistha* (installing the life force), a little *puja* and an *arati*. This may have been why all the papers were prepared so obligingly, and transporting the Supreme Lord was so easy. He was already present. And who could dare to say no to Lord Narasimhadeva?

The installation of Lord Narasimhadeva was very simple and lasted three days; from the 28th to the 30th of July, 1986. Atma Tattva Prabhu remembers feeling apprehensive that perhaps the installation was too simple. The grave warnings of the

Shankaracharya of Kanchipuram had left deep impressions. But soon it was apparent that everything was fine by the loud, dynamic *kirtana*, *sankirtana-yajna*, the only true opulence of Kali-yuga, that was dominating the scene. Everyone felt enlivened and satisfied. Lord Narasimhadeva, the protector of the *sankirtana* mission, had finally decided to manifest at Sri Mayapur Chandrodaya Mandir.

LORD NARASIMHADEVA RECIPROCATES INSTANTLY

Installing this Deity of Lord Narasimha in the temple was only the first step. What happens after the Deity is installed continues to show the presence of the personality of Lord Narasimha on a regular basis. So, here are a few stories as related by Pankajanghri das of Mayapur, the *pujari* or priest who takes care of the Deity, that shows how this Deity reveals Himself to His devotees.

As Pankajanghri das describes, I have been asked to recount some stories in connection with Him, the Deity of Lord Narasimhadeva, but unlike the *sastras* (scriptures), these "lilas" (pastimes) have no authority except for the testimony of the devotees who told them. In most cases there were no other witnesses. Although I am generally quite skeptical when it comes to accepting other people's mystical experiences as truth, just too many things started happening recently, not to sit up and take notice.

For instance, during one Gaura Purnima festival, I called over a devotee in the crowd and asked her to distribute the Lord's *charanamrita* [bathing water] to the ladies, which she did. Later, when she brought the *charanamrita* pot back, she remarked that Lord Narasimhadeva was very merciful to reciprocate so quickly.

"I was praying this morning that I might be able to offer some direct service to Him, and now you have given me this service."

"Yes," I said, "desires are quickly fulfilled in the holy *dham*. Just see, the same day you desire, it happened."

"No, not the same day--the same moment," she replied. "The very instant I expressed that desire to serve Him, you called me over."

"Wow! That is amazing," I acknowledged. "Did you hear about how one devotee's eye problem was cured at the same time that

The fierce but merciful Deity of Lord Narasimhadeva in Mayapur

Lord Narasimhadeva's original eyes were placed back, after one donor had bought Him new eyes?"

"Oh, yes," she told me. "As a matter of fact, I was staying in the same building when Lord Narasimhadeva spoke to her." She added, "You know, there was so much energy around that night that nobody could get any sleep."

Just a few days later, another devotee revealed how Lord Narasimhadeva helped him. "I was suffering intensely. I could not even stand without supporting myself on the column in front of Lord Narasimhadeva's altar. I prayed, 'Please help me. Take away this suffering condition so that I may serve You fully.' I then felt all my pain moving up and flowing out of my body. It just left."

While I was hearing this, I noticed another devotee who had come for the *darshan* of the Lord. Earlier in the morning this devotee had asked my advice what to do, for she had been afflicted for about two weeks with a severe problem that contaminated her body that wouldn't allow her to paint some Deities in Assam, although she had already been commissioned to do it and had an air ticket to go.

"Mataji," I exclaimed while walking over to her, "Lord Nrsimhadeva is giving instant benedictions. Why don't you ask Him to remove your problem?"

The very next morning, when she saw me, she said, "Thank you so much for the advice! You know, when I arrived home from the temple yesterday, my problem had completely disappeared."

Some days later another devotee came to the *pujari* room and told us about a dream, wherein Lord Narasimhadeva walked and talked with her just like a father. When she asked how she could serve Him, He told her to offer Him some mangoes. It wasn't the mango season, but she managed to get some, and we offered them for her. This was the year that His Holiness Gour Govinda Swami left his body in Mayapur.

A few days after this tragedy she came again and said, "Actually, I only told you half of the dream. Lord Narasimhadeva also said to me, "My *pujari* is very dear to Me, and I am going to take him back with Me.""

"Oh, don't do that, please," she fearfully exclaimed to the Lord. "We want him to stay here."

"No, I think I will take him back," He said.

"So after my pleading with Him for a long time, the Lord firmly announced. 'All right, then, I will take one of the gurus instead.'"

She concluded by saying, "I told my spiritual master about this dream, and he advised me not to tell anyone. But now, because it has come true, I think I can tell you."

When I repeated this story to my friend, Visvambhar from Carolina, he said, "This is amazing! My wife also dreamed about Lord Narasimhadeva and mangoes. You see, yesterday, while she was walking outside the Mayapur campus, she saw a jar of mango pickles in a shop and desired to buy them for Lord Narasimhadeva. But doubting the purity of the contents, she refrained. However, last night, Lord Narasimhadeva appeared in her dream and asked, "Where are My mango pickles?"

When Lord Narasimhadeva first came to Mayapur, all the *pujaris* were reluctant to worship His awesome form. Bhava Siddhi das was particularly frightened and always very nervous worshiping Him. One night, after putting the Lord to rest, he was leaving the altar when he heard such a tremendous sound that it made his hairs stand on end. Looking back fearfully, he saw that everything was in place. So he quickly left, locked the door and paid his obeisances, praying for forgiveness for any offense he might inadvertently have committed. At the end of that night he was awakened by the shaking of his bed. Bhava Siddhi was sleeping on the top of a bunk bed. So he thought it must be the *pujari* below him getting up for *mangala-arati* (morning worship).

However, when he opened his eyes, he saw Lord Narasimhadeva sitting on his bed. That fortunate *pujari* became very fearful, practically to the point of panic. As he tried to get up, Lord Narasimhadeva placed His two hands, which felt like the weight of the universe, on his shoulders. "Be peaceful, be calm," the Lord consoled him. "I have just come to tell you that when you worship

Me in the temple, there is no need to fear Me. Please, give up this fear."

The Lord then disappeared, but Bhava Siddhi began to run up and down the veranda of the Long Building, where he slept.

"What happened?" asked some concerned devotees. But they received only incoherent replies. They started to think maybe he had gone mad or become haunted by a ghost. Finally, Bhava Siddhi ran over to the temple and prostrated himself before the door where Lord Nrsimhadeva is worshiped and offered heartfelt prayers. After some time he became a little pacified, and began walking back to his room. "I wonder why everyone is staring at me," he thought. When he looked down, the answer was obvious: He had gone to the temple in his night dress.

I saw Bhava Siddhi at the Gaura Purnima festival--he was living in America--and asked him about that incident. "Yes," he said. "I still have those two marks from Lord Nrsimhadeva on my shoulders. They are almost gone now, but they are still visible."

He wasn't the only one to claim to have seen Lord Narasimhadeva. Once, a devotee from a nearby Gaudiya Math temple came to offer worship to Lord Narasimhadeva and told our head *pujari*, Jananivas, that on Narasimha Caturdasi (the Appearance Day of Narasimhadeva), he had been staying up all night chanting. Then, at the end of the night, Lord Narasimhadeva manifested Himself in his room. It was the form of Narasimhadeva from the Iskcon temple, and He appeared to be smiling very sweetly at me. My Guru Maharaj said I was very fortunate and should come here and worship Lord Narasimhadeva.

Another time the frantic parents of a runaway boy, after searching all over the country, finally heard that their son was at our Mayapur center. They immediately came and spent the whole day looking for him, inquiring at the reception desk and from individual devotees, but they were not at all lucky in tracing him.

At the end of the day, during the *sandhya arati* (evening worship) of Lord Narasimhadeva, his mother was praying with folded hands, "My dear Lord, the last time I came here, I happily participated in the chanting and dancing, but now my heart is broken because of my lost son, and I find no pleasure in life anymore. My Lord, if only my son could be returned to me, then I would also raise my hands and chant 'Haribol, Hare Krishna.'"

As these words left her mouth, a figure passed and stepped before her and Lord Narasimhadeva: it was her lost son. Both parents have now accepted Vaishnava initiation, started a *nama hatta* preaching center, and are enthusiastically preaching the Lord's glories.

There are other stories--some I would be hesitant to repeat, and others that I can't, having been told them in confidence. The devotees who told these stories have had their faith and conviction strengthened, and certainly mine was, too, by hearing them. So, if others derive the same benefit from reading them--even though they are not *sastra* (scripture)--it will be most beneficial. They help us advance in Krishna consciousness.

(These stories are just a few selections from http://narasimhalila.com/home.html, where you can find many more pastime descriptions)

Once, Lord Narasimhadev's worship in Mayapur was going on as usual when the *pujari* noticed that one flower fell from Narasimhadev's garland. The *pujari* asked the visitors if anyone was offering any special prayers to Lord Narasimhadev. The visitors in front did not say anything, but from the back one lady came forward with tears in her eyes. She said, "My daughter got married about four or five years ago and she has no issue. The people in my son-in-law's house consider it inauspicious. So I was praying to Narasimhadev that He might help her in her desperate situation." Then the *pujari* said, "Your prayer is granted, the symptom is that this flower fell from Narasimhadev's garland. Please take this and keep it nicely. You can wash this flower and give the water to your daughter to drink." Then the lady left, and later the *pujari* forgot the incident.

After one year, the same devotee, along with her daughter, son-in-law and a newborn baby came smiling to Narasimhadev. She reminded the *pujari* about the prayer she made one year back, as a result of which her daughter gave birth to a very nice baby boy, whom they named Prahlad. And once again they offered a very nice *puja* (offering) to Lord Narasimhadev.

(From http://narasimhalila.com/pastimes1.html)

MIRACLES IN MAYAPUR

To show further examples about the miracles that can take place with Krishna Deities, here are two little stories that relate how Deities can intercede and change the health and recovery of those who have been injured. This is again in regard to Lord Krishna's form as Lord Narasimhadeva, but it also exemplifies the sincerity of the people involved and the power of the faithful *pujaris*, such as Jananivas das and Pankajanghri das who have become famous simply for their devotion and dedication to the Deities in Mayapur. And I take great pleasure in helping spread examples that show the potency, glories and mercy of the Deities in this way. The following story is told with gratitude and love by Racitambara dasi.

On April 22, 2005, Revati Sundari devi dasi, age 8, was climbing on the roof of the bamboo playhouse in the Grihastha park in Sri Mayapur *dham*. To her great surprise she fell through the roof, landing on her head, and the roof caved in on top of her. She was in shock for an hour, shaking and crying and incoherent. She also had concussion. Gaura Baba, our wonderful homeopathic Vaishnava doctor, treated her for concussion and shock and suggested a scan.

After three days, Revati woke up in the night vomiting black blood. We rushed her off to Kolkata. On the way, clear fluid was leaking from her nose, then violent nosebleeds started.

We took her straight to a good pediatrician, who immediately called in the top neurologist in the city. He ordered a CT scan and then, seeing the results, he sent us to a very good neurosurgeon, who has his own private hospital. Revati was admitted straight away.

The symptoms continued through the night, and we found out that the clear fluid from her nose was the brain fluid (CFS) leaking out. The scan clearly showed a fracture in the floor of her brain, from which the brain fluid was escaping. Also her brain was swollen and blood was pooling there, causing pressure. She had extreme pain in her head which was unabated since the accident. The doctors worked on her for a couple of days, giving her medicine intravenously. The whites of her eyes became totally red. She was like a limp rag with little interest in anything.

Finally the doctors said that the next morning, early, they would do a special scan showing all the sections of her brain to determine the exact extent of the injuries and then would probably decide to operate to repair the damage. They would tell us their decision by 9 am.

I phoned Pankajanghri Prabhu, explaining the situation and asking him to please pray to Lord Nrsimhadev. He immediately said he would do a full *puja* (offering) between 5 and 7 am, complete with *abhisekha* (bathing ceremony) and everything else. This was the time of the special scan.

The next morning when I met the doctors, they were looking amazed and said that the new scan showed that the injuries were miraculously almost healed. All the symptoms such as pain, violent nosebleeds, brain fluid leakage, vomiting, etc., had abruptly stopped.

When I went in to see Revati, she was sitting up in bed looking bright-eyed and fresh, and her eyes were fully white again. Thank you, Lord Nrsimhadev!

Another example is that on October 28th, 2006, Chakravarty Raj, the 14 year old son of Radha Kanta Gopal das and Padma Radhika devi dasi was injured when a fire cracker burst in his face. He was immediately rushed to hospital. The doctors said that he suffered from 2nd degree burn injuries on his face and suggested (1) facial dressing immediately, (2) chemical crafting after a fortnight and then (3) plastic surgery after 6 months or 1 year.

Next morning, the parents requested Pankajanghri Prabhu to offer special offerings to Lord Narasimhadev for the speedy recovery of Chakravarty Raj, which were duly performed.

For the next 2 days, he was just lying in bed without much movement. He could not even open his eyelids. He was then taken to

Disha eye hospital at Barackpur, where they found that the carina (the white portions of the eyes) took the burn injury and the pupils were unharmed. Hence, there would be no problem with his sight and a treatment of 15 days would cure the carina.

On 2nd November morning, Padma Radhika devi dasi approached her Guru Mahraja, His Holiness Jayapataka Swami, and told him of what had happened. He gestured that he will pray for him and applied Narasimha oil on her forehead. The same morning, Chakra was taken to Kolkata for treatment of his facial injuries

After getting an opinion at the Apollo Hospital in the morning, Chakravarty was taken to the Railway Hospital at Howrah. One of the senior Doctors tested him and confirmed that it was a second degree burn and sent him to the dressing room for initial facial dressing. But within 3 minutes one of the staff from the dressing room rushed out yelling and took the parents inside. Upon seeing Chakravarty the parents stood there motionless, struck with wonder and amazement. There was Chakra, standing and smiling, with no trace of any injury or mark on his face!! Narasimhadev ki jai!!

When asked for clarification, the doctor and others present in that place could not give any valid reason. One of them said, "You can go back in your temple and ask you Lord about it. *Yeh tho apke Bhagavan ka chamarkar hai.* This is your Lord's miracle."

LORD NARASIMHA IN SOUTH AFRICA

Here is a true story that happened in 1998 in South-Africa. The father and the daughter who experienced this event told this story to a friend, a sannyasi and devotee of Lord Narasimhadev. This story was also found in the newspapers, and several witnesses of this truck-accident after this incident became devotees of Lord Narasimhadev.

This happened to a simple Vaishnava family that lives there. They had a 5-year old daughter. This girl was a great "fan" of Lord Narasimhadeva, she found Him simply funny, as he looked half-lion and half-man and felt very attracted to Him. She often told her playmates about her favorite God, a lion, and the kids always wondered about what kind of God this could be.

What can a five year old girl know about God? She wasn't initiated, not even her parents Although the father of the family followed a guru and was close to a small Hindu-community.

What happened was that one day the girl was playing outside with her ball along with some other kids near the street. The ball, however, landed in the street, and the girl ran after her precious ball. There was hardly any traffic on this rarely used country road. But this time a very fast truck came running down the way. The girl in her play didn't see the truck coming.

The father was in the first floor of the house and saw his baby girl running on the street, but he also saw the huge truck coming, closing in on his daughter with great speed. The father yelled at her, but she didn't hear him. So he jumped out of the window to save his daughter and broke both his legs, laying on the ground in pain.

Then, helpless, he had to watch how his little girl was hit by the truck and thrown through the air, landing some 20 meters away. All of the children and neighbors around who observed this froze with shock. The father later said that when he saw this his only desire was to die.

From the other direction came a police car that also witnessed the accident. The truck went on and the policeman drove his car across the street to stop him. The truck-driver was barely able to stop his truck and seemed to be very drunk. The policeman immediately called the ambulance and ran over to the motionless girl laying in the grass. The closest hospital was a small private clinic. The ambulance came, but refused to take the girl, being afraid they wouldn't have the necessary machines to help the injuries the girl must have. They advised the policeman to call the main hospital, as only they could efficiently help her, as they suspected that her spine must be broken, etc. The policeman was in despair, not even knowing where the father of the girl was. Actually, he didn't even know if the girl was still alive, and he didn't dare to touch her, not knowing how injured she was. However, in the end she was brought to a good hospital, and the policeman accompanied the girl, along with her father who also arrived there.

The chief-doctor heard what had happened to the girl, and

they immediately X-rayed her to see the results. The policeman wanted to be assured of how the girl was doing, and waited to see the results. Everybody was shocked to hear of what a terrific accident that had happened to the girl.

However, when the nurse brought the X-ray pictures to the doctor, he became very upset and started yelling at the nurse that she should, for-God's sake, at least bring the right pictures. After all, this was about life or death. He even threatened to fire her, as it was unacceptable to make such mistakes. The nurse was scared and didn't understand what was happening. Yet, those were the correct pictures of the five year old girl who had been hit by the truck. The nurse wasn't aware yet of what had happened to the girl. When the doctor viewed the X-rays, he said that they could not be the right pictures because they showed that there was not a single broken bone. The doctor kept saying all the time, again and again, that it was impossible, it can't be.

Then suddenly the girl awoke from her faint and, in full awareness, told a story which made its tour through the media.

She explained that in the moment she picked up the ball from the street, she saw the truck coming up to her. And the only thing she could do was to yell out for help. She didn't call for mommy or daddy, but for her Narasimhadev. In that moment, when the truck hit her, she suddenly saw how Narasimhadev picked her up from the ground, smiled at her, and said, "Don't be afraid, nothing will happen to you." The girl continued her story that the Lord had put her on the other side of the street into the grass. But when putting her down, He accidentally scratched her waist, which still hurt her a bit.

She spoke about how beautiful Narasimhadev was, His hair, His eyes, etc., but his claws were very sharp and He should cut them. She also spoke about how He wore a golden dhoti, etc. The doctor didn't understand anything and told the policeman she still was in shock and hallucinated, which is normal.

So, the girl was profoundly checked for any injuries, but the only injury they found on her body were those scratches. The doctor said this must be from a wild animal like a lion, as he had cases like this before. So, he was disturbed and asked if they had been the ones who brought the girl to hospital since she was injured by a wild animal, not a truck. Nobody was clear on how to explain it. However, later the same doctor and nurse who took care of her became devotees after they learned from the parents who "that lion" was.

So, as we can see, miracles still happen today. These are not mere stories from the *Mahabharata, Puranas* or *shastras* that are thousands of years old. This was simply because the little girl was very attracted to this form of God, and in her despair she called Him for help. Lord Narasimhadev did not consider if she was initiated or had the right to call His name. He protects His devotees that sincerely worship Him in their hearts.

The little girl was obviously no common soul, and who can say what she did in her previous life to have such an experience.

SRI SRI RADHA GANDHARVIKA GIRIDHARI IN MAYAPUR

At the Sri Caitanya Math, on Bhaktisiddhanta Road a few kilometres North of Iskcon Mayapur, the Deities here were personally installed and worshiped by Srila Bhaktisiddhanta Saraswati Thakur.

As it was told by Vrajanath Prabhu, from the Sevak office in Iskcon Mayapur, there was one maker of Deities in Jaipur who had a dream. He had many finished Deities, but one particular Deity appeared to him in the dream and said, "Tomorrow my very great devotee will come to take me away."

The next day, Srila Bhaktisiddhanta Saraswati visited the Deity maker looking for Deities. The man immediately took Srila Bhaktisiddhanta to the Deities and said, "Here are your Deities."

When Srila Bhaktisiddhanta Saraswati asked why he had said these were his Deities, the Deity maker told him about the dream. Srila Bhaktisiddhanta joyfully accepted the Deities and worshiped them for the rest of his life. This happened in 1922.

He named them Sri Sri Gandharvika Giridhari. The name *Gandharvika* means, "She who sings like a Gandharva" meaning Her voice is so sweet, like a Gandharva, which indicates Srimati Radharani. And *Giridhari*, as you know, is the one who lifted Govardhan Hill.

THE BALA GOPALA DEITY AND
KRISHNA PREMA DAS

Krishna Prema (Ronald Noxon) served for a time as a priest or *pujari* in the temple of Bala Gopala, the Deity of his guru, Yashoda Ma in Mirtola, a village in the Himalayas. One night while asleep, Krishna Prema heard someone calling "Dada, Dada." He suddenly got up and looked around but saw no one. Thinking that it was nothing, he again closed his eyes and laid down. But again he heard the sweet call "Dada," meaning elder brother. This time he could understand that it came from inside the temple. But no one was inside. So how could this be? Yes, as he went near the temple he heard, "Dada, I am feeling cold. The window is open."

Then Krishna Prema went into the temple and found that the window was indeed open. So he closed the window and carefully covered the body of Bala Gopala with a quilt. When he said, "Thakura, You feel so cold," a stream of tears flowed from the eyes of the Deity, making Krishna Prema feel petrified. But here was the Supreme Lord accepting the position of the child Deity who was completely dependent on the loving care of his "Dada," wanting to be loved and enjoy this sweet, intimate relationship between them.

KICKED BY THE KARTAMASHA DEITY

As told by Pusta Krishna Prabhu: When I first came to Krishna consciousness movement in Gainesville, Florida in 1970, I had never seen an ISKCON temple. I took one Hinduism course which showed a movie about Deity worship of Sri Sri Radha Krishna in India. I remember going back to speak with Gargamuni Swami and I asked him if he did that also. He said "Yes". Coming from the Jewish tradition where idolatry was frowned upon, I was uneasy. So, in February 1971, we started our hitch-hiking trip up to New York, on the way to East Pakistan on Srila Prabhupada's orders. When I first arrived in the Brooklyn temple, it was night-time. The following morning, I went to my first *mangala-aratik*. I was really shaken seeing the odd forms of the Jagannath Deities. I had literally joined the movement under a tree in the Plaza of the Americas in Gainesville.

Anyway, the years passed, I took sanyasa in 1972 at age 22. Some months later, I was at the Los Angeles Temple. The current temple room was then the old church with pews. At the front of the room was the single Deity of Kartamasha, Krishna as an elephant herds boy. While I was taking rest one afternoon, that Kartamasha Deity appeared in my dream. I looked down at His lotus feet and noticed He was making circles with His big toe. I thought to myself, "the Deity can't move His toe!" I bent down in my dream to take a closer look, and He kicked me in the head with His foot!!! I was immediately transported to the Brahman plane, very laughingly liberating knowing that my Lord had such a wonderful and charming sense of humor. Needless to say, I never looked upon another Deity the same way again. Although They may stand still on the altar…I know They do so at Their own sweet will, being capable of wonderful activities if They so choose.

SAVED BY GAURA NITAI

This story is from Malati devi dasi, a disciple of Srila A. C. Bhaktivedanta Prabhupada who had helped start the Hare Krishna Movement in Europe. She relates, as recorded in class at Detroit in April, 2011: At one point I was in charge of a group of ladies traveling and doing book distribution in Belgium and Holland. We had a wonderful set-up inside a Mercedes van with installed Deities of Sri Sri Gaura Nitai (Lord Chaitanya and Nityananda). So we would have a regular morning program for Them in the van and then the whole day we were out distributing books. Then we would come back in the evening and see the Deities again and then go to sleep. A simple life, and very blissful.

However, it was one winter in Holland in which they said it was the coldest winter in 53 years. So we would sleep in our sleeping bags and coats and we were still cold in that van. So we went to a camping store and purchased a heater, and we were really excited that we were finally going to be warm. So we looked around and I found a place under some trees to park the van for the night where there were no houses around. Then, in anticipation, that evening we closed the windows to make sure they were really tightly closed so we would not lose one bit of heat. And we happily went to sleep that night.

Later, after I had been asleep for a while, I saw myself in a dream lying on a road. And I saw Sri Sri Gaura Nitai coming down the road, but when They came to me They started kicking me in the side. And They were saying, "Get up! Get up! It's time for *mangala arati*, get up!" And I was feeling Them kicking me in my side, and so I tried to wake up, but I couldn't wake up, and I realized something was wrong. Now it was no longer a dream, I was trying to get up but I couldn't get up. I was sleeping by the door and I managed to get the door opened and I rolled out onto the ground.

That night it had snowed so I fell into the snow and as my head started to clear, I started pulling the other women out of the van yelling, "Get out! Get out of the van!" One of the women were saying, "Leave me alone, I don't want to get up now." And I responded by saying, "Get out! You have to get out now, something is wrong!" And we all had these horrible, horrible headaches.

So, to make a long story short, by closing the windows there was no oxygen, and the heater had burned up all the oxygen. So, if Gaura Nitai had not come and woke me up, we would have all died. It was the Deities who saved us.

Then, a funny part of the story, the police came and surrounded us with dogs. The police were all speaking in Dutch and none of us spoke Dutch, except for Hello, and Good Day, just enough to get by. It turned out the place where I parked was a place where they trained the dogs, the K-9 forces. So they saw us there wondering what is going on. When they realized what had happened, they took us right away to a hospital to be checked out. We got better, but it was Gaura Nitai who saved our lives that day. But as I look back on it, it was so amazing and so wonderful to be kicked in the side by the lotus feet of Sri Sri Gaura Nitai.

The Little Lord Jagannatha Deities (Lord Balarama, Lady Subhadra and Lord Jagannatha) of Chintamani devi dasi

LORD BALARAMA SHOWS HIS PRESENCE

This is told by Chintamani devi dasi, who helped open the first Hare Krishna temple in Japan. As she explains:

Little Lord Jagannatha, Little Lord Balarama and Lady Subhadra, as They are lovingly called (all about 10 inches tall), arrived at the Japan temple in 1970. I don't know where They came from, probably from somewhere in India. I just remember that we opened a box we got in the mail and there He was, with Little Lord Balarama and Lady Subhadra. We made an altar for Them and started doing *aratis* and offering food, although we did not have any clothes for Them.

I'll describe one special incident that involves Little Lord Jagannatha. In Japan, we had Lord Jagannatha on a little altar and there was no one else in the house we used as a temple. One day I was cooking the offering, and the offerings in Japan were pretty much on time, but they weren't exact. On this occasion I was cooking and I was thinking, "Is Lord Jagannatha really eating this food? How do I know He is really eating this food?"

I happened to be late for the offering and I heard a noise come from another part of the house, like a thud. Although I knew there was no one else in the house, I stopped for a minute. But then I kept cooking and about a minute later I heard the same noise again. Then I was scared and wondered what it was, and whether somebody else was in the house that I didn't know about. So I looked in the front room and the back room of this tiny Japanese house, and then I looked in the temple room and saw Lord Balarama standing on the bottom shelf of the altar, which was three shelves high. I wondered how He had gotten there. It was as if He took two steps down. Then the only thought that was in my mind was that maybe He was hungry because I was late for the offering and maybe He was trying to show me He was eating it.

So I put Lord Balarama back up on the altar and went back to the kitchen and finished the offering really fast to keep the Deities from waiting. When the brahmacharis came back from *sankirtana*, I told them what happened but they just looked at each other like, "Yeah, sure." But that's what appeared to happen.

This is just one of many other incidents that have happened with these particular Deities that she will be glad to tell you if you see her. Due to the mercy of Srila Prabhupada, these Deities became Chintamani's personal Deities in 1972 when he ordered her to take Them wherever she went.

LORD JAGANNATHA IN LONDON SOHO

One time the *pujaris* were preparing to offer a flower set to Sri Sri Radha London-Isvara (Radha & Krishna). This means that the whole outfit of the Deities are made of flowers. A donor had offered the funds required.

Then that night while one of the *pujaris* was sleeping, Lord Jagannath appeared to her in a dream. He said, "I am God just as much as He is! I want a flower set also."

"But Lord Jagannath," she pleaded nervously, "Someone donated the money for the flower set. We don't have the money to buy a flower set for You."

"Don't worry," Lord Jagannath said. "Radharani will arrange everything."

Then the next day someone came to the temple and donated the money needed to buy Lord Jagannath's flowers, and the devotees enthusiastically prepared a flower set for Lord Jagannath as well.

A FEW STORIES BY ANJU KEJRIWAL

Anju is from Bombay and was raised in a spiritual family, so she always had Balgopal (the Deity of child Krishna) in the house and they would serve Him. She explains:

I have got a small Balgopal at home and one time a friend got some laddu sweets, and she started opening them. But I said "No, no. Let me do an offering of them to my Balgopal, and then we can all take." And then she said "You and your Krishna," like she was laughing at me.

Then she came into my temple room and she asked "Does Krishna really eat?"

I replied, "Of course He eats. How can you say He does not eat?" Even from my childhood we always accepted that Krishna eats through His Deity. But my friend thought I was crazy, but I said nonetheless, let me do the offering.

She had come to stay with us, and the next day she was sleeping where my Deity room was and she got up in the morning and she was praying there a little bit, and then she herself saw two laddu crumbs on the clothes of my Balgopal Krishna Deity. And then she called me to come and see. She said, I don't believe your Krishna eats. But the evidence was there, so she saw this herself and became convinced. And then she looked at the laddus herself that were left in the bowl and she could see like two little teeth had pricked the laddus where Krishna would have taken a few bites out of them, before the crumbs were on His clothes. So then her faith started to build up, and she decided that I was not totally mad.

Another time I went out of town. I give my Deity of Balgopal hot milk every night. My maids were in the house and they were alone, but they knew the routine to give the Deity offerings. If I'm not there, then my daughter would do it, or even the maids would do it.

So when I got back from out of town my maid told me, "Your Krishna is real." So I asked what happened. She said that she forgot to give Them milk in the night. She explained, "At 2 A.M. in the night He was kicking me and telling me to 'Give Me milk.'" The maids were busy watching TV because no one else was there. So they did not give the Deities milk but He woke her up and told her to "Give Me milk." Then she got up and give Him some hot milk.

So when I got back she was so scared and said that your Krishna is real. I said "See, He is not just stone. So whatever we eat, we first feed Him."

RADHA-KRISHNA IN MY DREAMS

This is told by Madhava Lata devi dasi from Italy. She explains:

I saw myself in a huge temple room, and there were many, many devotees. Some were chanting, others were talking, walking, admiring the Deities. The Deities were on this big altar but not very much raised from the floor level, just one step, and without any sort of boundaries. They were completely dressed and bedecked in white and also made of white marble, but they were actually moving. Krishna was bent as usual in His *tribanga* (three curved bending) form, but instead of holding the flute He had in one hand (His right) a long little box, and in the other hand a thin brush. He was putting on kajjhal, and with a sidelong glance He was looking into the little mirror that Radharani was holding for Him. Also, Radharani was holding a mirror in her right hand, and looking into it with the side of her eye and shyly giggling. So while Krishna was putting on the kajjhal, They were playfully looking into each others eyes in the little hand-mirror.

Many devotees were uttering exclamations of delight and joy at this pastime of the Divine Couple. I was also watching but I was taken by so much emotion that tears were coming down from my eyes, so I started to walk towards the side door because I did not want the devotees to see my emotions. But there were so many of them that I had difficulties in making my way through the crowd, so much so that I fell down long on the floor. Then I started to crawl towards the door with difficulty since I was blinded by my tears and, when I made it, on the doorway stood the same Radha-Krishna in the same white dress, but there They were entwined in a dance. At that point I just put my head on their Lotus Feet.

I always think and meditate on this form of the Lord, even though I never read of this pastime, at least in my limited knowledge. I have also found a name to remember this pastime as Sri Sri Radha Kajjhal Kanu. I don't even know if this is correct in Sanskrit, but it reminds me of the mood of the Lord in this pastime. Now it is two years that I am thinking of having a painting made depicting this vision.

SAVED FROM NIGHTMARES BY BALARAMA

I used to have nightmares in black and white, all of my life (til teen-age) about being chased, living in a war zone, etc. Then after reading the "Krishna" book regularly every night before bedtime for several days (70s trilogy), one night I had a dream in which Balarama slammed his mace and then suddenly ever after that I would dream in color and never had those hellish type of dreams again. (From a person who preferred to be anonymous)

BALARAMA WINKS

I had been chanting *japa* meditation for maybe one-and-a-half to two years while I was a *brahmacharini* in the temple and had recently come to the San Francisco temple in 1971. We were reading from the *Nectar of Devotion* in the morning, and we read the story of Lord Balarama drinking His *varuni* honey beverage and becoming intoxicated. When I read this, I was so amazed, and I asked in my heart to Lord Balarama on the altar there, "Is our Lord Balarama really here?"

Then He winked one of His huge lotus eyes to let me know it was indeed Him. It was a huge, huge wink. Jaya Jaya Lord Balarama!

Many years later - more than 20 years ago, I had lent my small Jagannath Deities (about 8 inches tall) to someone but had done so with the caveat that I might ask for Them back sometime when I was able to care for Them. Finally, my life had settled, and I asked for the Deities back (how They arrived to me in the first place is another story). The person didn't remember that I had only "loaned" Jagannath, Balarama and Subhadra to them. I begged and pleaded to no avail. Several years went by. I could not forget my Deities. So finally, one day my husband and I got in our car and drove the 400 miles to where the Deities were - on a shelf as decorations, not on an altar - and "stole" Them, replacing Them with other new and similar Deities. We were so scared someone would catch us, but the adults of the house were not in the room.

We quickly drove off feeling like the worst sinners and criminals but I was forced from inside to do this. On our way up the mountains, the full moon started to rise behind the clouds and naturally I was praying to Krishna for protection and forgiveness if I had done wrong. Then the clouds opened up some holes - the exact replica of Lord Jagannath's beautiful face appeared in the clouds - two large round eyes and one perfect big smile underneath; except one of the large eyes was half closed in a wink. This lasted just for a minute or two. Amazing, but absolutely true. (From Anonymous)

THE HUNTER'S BLESSING

This recipient of Krishna's mercy was a hunter residing in Nigeria, Africa and this is a recent incident. One morning the hunter drew an arrow in his bow to shoot a bird. Just as he did this, he actually heard a clear, loud voice say: "Don't do that."

He complied with the voice and ceased to shoot. Then later that night, he had a dream where he was directed by a man to visit a temple in another African city, maybe South Africa. He again obliged the direction and went to visit that temple. As soon as he arrived, he was astonished to recognize the man from his dream, Srila Prabhupada, sitting high as a *murti*, or image. In fact, as soon as he entered the temple, he was stunned and immediately shouted out his discovery: "That's the man from my dream." With such a startling introduction to Krishna and the mercy of the pure devotee, he stopped his hunting and is now becoming a devotee. (This story was described by His Holiness Bhakti Vasudeva Swami.)

SRI GOVINDAJI RECIPROCATES

One of my miracles with Krishna occurred very early in my devotee career. Though I lived outside the temple at the time, as well as most times in my devotional life, I'd quickly acquired the habit of attending the *mangala arati* and found the whole atmosphere of the (early morning) *brahma muhurta* period simply enchanting. This was taking place in the Brooklyn, New York temple, and because the *kirtans* there were so exquisite and energetic, my ecstasy was almost uncontainable. Because of this, I soon began skipping across the whole width of the temple, maybe 20 or 25 feet, and I'd usually do this at top speed. Having been an athlete most of my life, this was done pretty fast. I was in such ecstasy in fact that I'd just go back and forth, skipping rapidly across the floor to release my reverie and hopefully, if I could, please the Lord.

I can't say exactly how or when, but pretty soon after I started doing this, I noticed that one of the Deities on the altar was skipping along with me. I could actually see this with my peripheral vision, and I was totally flabbergasted seeing this, but also very thrilled and so enlivened. Doubters will of course doubt this testimony, but I could care less. I don't doubt it because I saw with my own eyes the shadow of a large Deity moving across the floor with me at about the same speed. I was very far away from the altar, because I always did this in the very rear of the temple where I hoped no one would see me, but there's no doubt in my mind that the shadow and figure I saw moving across the altar with me was none other than the Deity of Sri Govindaji, who reciprocated my excitement. (By Raga Devi Dasi)

TRANSPORTED TO GOLOKA VRINDAVANA

I recall one night I was immediately "implanted" in Goloka Vrndavana. All I could experience was unlimited pure living entities chanting or actually vibrating the holy name with their entire beings. I was surrounded by them, like being in an ocean and I was one particle, also chanting with all my being. I recall that everyone was very, very excited as "Krsna and Balarama are coming!" There was a mood of ever-increasing happiness – that the transcendental brothers were coming. There was an intensity and heightened expectation that increased again and again and again. The intensity continued to rise and so did the happiness. That was a simultaneous understanding, along with the complete "immersion" of all entities in vibrating the holy name. There was ever-increasing bliss with no cessation, simply increasing, increasing, increasing. I did not get to wait until They came, as the experience also ended abruptly.

Again, I did not "see" anything, but understood I was "experiencing" transcendental activity amongst the pure souls in the spiritual world.

Conclusion: I have absolutely no qualification for any of these experiences, and it has been over 10 years since these events occurred. However, I have been fortunate enough to have been given a glimpse of reality and that keeps me going in my darkest hours. I have not made these experiences widely known, due to them being easily misunderstood. However, I hope that some people may gain strength from what I experienced. My final conclusion of the entirety of these events is that Krishna Consciousness is for each of us, not just for the pure souls in the Vedic literature. Krishna has come, Lord Chaitanya has come, Srila Prabhupada has come for each and every one of us to go back home. What we read about can be experienced by us, by the grace of the devotees of the Lord, guru and Krishna. This philosophy is not merely theoretical, neither is it exaggeration. If it happened to me, let me assure, it can happen to anyone as I am no one special. I am not saying this out of humility, it is just a simple fact. Please take heart that you can also be transferred to the spiritual world, in this very life, and that the spiritual world is very real, and that Srila Prabhupada is unlimitedly merciful. (Preferred anonymous)

STORIES OF A FAMILY'S SPIRITUAL BLESSINGS

Here is a story from a family in Metro Detroit in which they explain the series of events that propelled them along in their spiritual development. They now conclude that these events are the direct blessings of the Deities. The wife first tells her part:

Some years ago, before we became involved in Krishna consciousness or bhakti-yoga, we had been married for about 8 to 9 years. So I was finishing my fellowship and my husband had just finished and was working really hard, doing as many cases as possible, even if someone called him at two in the morning. Someone told him that you have to make yourself very approachable and available to make a surgeon's practice flourish. So he was starting completely new. So it was a very hectic and stressful lifestyle for both of us. So under that stress we started arguing more and reached a stage where we were not very happy with each other. So things started going bad until things could take a turn for the worse.

So on January 1, 2007 we went to a New Year's Party. I was wearing an overcoat and just before leaving, I took out a picture of Radha-Kunjabihari from my pocket. My in-laws would go to the temple once in a while and gave the picture to me, and I had that. So when the people started wishing everyone else a happy new year, I took out the picture and prayed and asked for a good year. But starting from that day, things just got worse between us. So it reached a point where the marriage had to improve or it just wasn't going to last.

Six months later I got a job at the hospital and was doing research for a month. So I was able to leave early and do other things. So on the way back home I would stop by the temple, not because I was so attracted to it, or knew that this is where I would be later in life, but just because it was convenient. I could not settle myself anywhere else, so I would stop there at the temple. Usually the *darshan* of the main Deities would be closed at the time I would often arrive, so I would sit in front of Sri Nathji and the Lakshmi-Narayana Deities and cry to Them, or lament in my heart that things are not going right and that something has to happen for things to get better, or ask "Why are you doing this to me?" So that went on for a few months when I would just stop in and see the Deities, or sit in the main hall in front of Radha-Kunjabihari even if the curtains were closed. So it wasn't like love for Krishna, but I was asking Them to do something.

Then I met the wife of one of the devotees who was working in the same office as I was. I never knew she was into Krishna Consciousness, and we would only talk business. Then one day she asked me if I wanted to go to a program at someone's home. And I really did not think I would want to go to someone's home on a weekend just because of one invitation. Later, on the day of the event, she called me to see if I was interested, so I asked my husband and he said sure. I was pretty convinced that he wouldn't go, and I don't know what made him say yes. So we went, and when we got there, one devotee was giving a talk on "Who am I." And it was very nice, and we became very interested in the whole philosophy.

Then, while talking to my friend at work, she asked if I want to come for Krishna Janmastami (the festival of Krishna's appearance). They were going to New Vrindavana in West Virginia, and would we like to go. But I was thinking no, I don't think we would go to a temple for a weekend vacation, and driving so far and all of that. So I said that I would ask my husband, and again he said sure. Maybe it would be good to get out of the house for a bit. So we went, and that's when things really began to happen in our spiritual development.

Now when I look back, I realize that when I was at the temple in front of the Deities, asking the Deities why are You doing this to me, and asking Them to change things and make things better, that is when the transition started and progressed to the point where I'm now at the temple every weekend doing service to the Deities, and I'm attached to the temple, and things are so much nicer and good now. So I think it is the Deities' direct mercy that we are now in this process of spiritual development. And people think that things with us in our marriage are perfect, and now they are perfect. I just cannot imagine how things could be so bad and now things are so good, and things could change so much.

Now when I see others struggling with things like that, I can completely understand and I try to help if I can. I think others go through the same thing. But we were very blessed to get this kind of spiritual association.

Now the husband explains how things continued:

My first Deity pastime begins in the year 2007. This was during the Janmastami celebration when we first got involved in Krishna Consciousness. That is when we made our first visit to the New Vrindavan temple. When we went to view the Narasimha Deity, I was amazed at the Deity, how big He was, but there was a large crowd in front of the Deity and I could not get close enough to get a good view. So I was wishing for a better view of the Deity. Then suddenly the flames of the *arati* lamp fell in front of the crowd, and everybody just scattered and moved out of the way. That allowed me the room to just move up in front of the Deity and get a good, clear *darshan*. So Lord Narasimha created a situation and granted my wish to see Him.

The very next day they had a *japa* session to teach people how to chant the Hare Krishna mantra after *mangala arati*. So as everybody was leaving the temple room in a line, there was one devotee who was handing out beads to chant on, if anyone was interested. That was before I had started chanting. So I was thinking, "Oh, chanting. We don't need this chanting." So I was thinking I will not take the beads. So he was asking everyone if they wanted beads. But when I got up to him, he didn't even ask me, he just handed them to me. So I said, "How come you are asking everyone but you are not asking me?"

So I stood there looking at him and he looked at me. So he asked, "You want beads?" and I answered "OK."

Then he said, "Sixteen rounds." So that's when I started chanting 16 rounds daily, that same day.

The next pastime was during Krishna Janmastami in 2008 here in Detroit at the Hare Krishna temple. So by now I was really into it. It was a weekday for the festival, which went on until after 12:30 at night. But the next day I knew I had a very busy schedule with a major 6 to 8 hour surgery to perform, and I had to be in the hospital by 7:30 AM. So I needed to be fresh and clear-headed. I had been in the temple until 10 PM that night, and I just felt really bad leaving, but it was a major operation that I was expected to do and I didn't want to be drowsy. So I had this tussle in my mind, do I operate or do I stay at the festival until one or two AM and just take a chance that I will be all right. I thought Krishna would be happy if I just went home early and did my karma, or what I was duty-bound to do.

So just as I walked into the house there was a voicemail from my assistant saying that he could not be there for me tomorrow. So that was easy, because if he could not be there, I cannot do the operation. Then I called my patient and told him that I am without my assistant and you don't want me to do the operation without my assistant, so we have to reschedule. So I went right back to the temple just in time for the Janmastami celebration. In this way, Sri Sri Radha-Kunjabihari granted my wish.

Their son tells this pastime of how their own Deities of Gaura-Nitai came to their house.

It was a few weeks before we were going to Mayapur and it had been a year-and-a-half since we had taken up bhakti-yoga, Krishna consciousness, and many of our friends already had Deities in their homes. So I was asking my parents why don't we have Deities, and they said we'll get Them when the time comes, when Krishna thinks we are ready. So I said "OK."

When we reached Mayapur, it was during Radhanatha Swami's *yatra*. So I was asking if this wasn't the perfect place and situation to get Deities?

Then the day before we left India, we were coming back home from the *yatra*, all the devotees from Michigan were scheduled to meet with Radhanatha Swami. There were also ten to fifteen sets of Deities lined up on a bench outside the ashrama where Swamiji was staying so he could come out, meet the devotees, and then give names to all these sets of Gaura-Nitai Deities that the devotees would take back with them.

Then one devotee, Yugal Kishore, told everyone to hold their Deities when Swamiji would give names for Them, and we held one set of Deities as well, even though we had not purchased any set for ourselves, and the ones we were holding were actually meant for Yugal Kishore's mother. Then when Radhanatha Swami was coming down the line, giving each set of Deities Their name, he came to us and asked my father, "Is this set of Deities for you?"

He said , "Yes." He couldn't say no.

He said, "OK, these Deities are for you, and they are Sri Sri Nitai-Mayapur Bihari."

So, after all the Deities got names, we had to tell Yugal Kishore that these are our Deities now, because Swamiji confirmed it. So my desire to have Deities was fulfilled.

After that, we took the Deities into the main temple room to show Them to the main Deities of Pancha-Tattva and to Srila Prabhupada, since it was also the observance of Srila Prabhupada's disappearance day. And then so many of the local devotees just thronged us, lined up to see our new Deities saying how beautiful They were.

Then in the evening we went to Srila Prabhupada's *samadhi* for kirtan, but it was so packed with people that we decided to better use our time to get some Deity outfits before we leave Mayapur. While we were shopping, Radhanatha Swami had come out of the *samadhi* and saw us, stopped, said some kind words, and then gave us the garland he was wearing, which had come from the Deity of Srila Prabhupada in the *samadhi*. So that was very special, and we still have that garland to this day.

The husband now continues to relate some of the additional pastimes that have happened. These are just a few.

Many pastimes have happened since we have acquired our Deities. I was chanting my rounds in front of my Deities one morning, and I had to be at the hospital fairly early. So I knew I would not be able to finish my rounds of *japa* meditation before I had to leave, and the day was so busy that I knew I would not be able to get back to it until 10 PM at night in order to finish. So I was asking the Deities if there was something They could do so I could simply finish my rounds of *japa*, chanting the Hare Krishna mantra. I had to be at the hospital by 9 AM, but I called the operating room at 7:45 AM to see what the status of my case was, and the person says, "Your case got canceled, did you know?"

I said, "Really? I never canceled it."

So I called the patient and asked if he canceled, but he said, "No. Your office called to cancel it."

I replied, "My office does not open until 8:30, and I never told my office to cancel it." And there is only one other lady besides me in my office, and she won't do anything like that without confirmation from me. So how did that happen? My Deities answered my prayers again. So I was able to go and finish my rounds of *japa* meditation very nicely.

This next pastime was in regard to the nice programs we just had with Radhanatha Swami while he was here in Detroit, 2011. I always spend some time with my own Gaura Nitai Deities before I go to bed. I had really wanted the program to be at the Grosse Pointe War Memorial because the venue is good, location is nice, and I thought everyone would like it. So I went there to ask how to book the facilities, but the lady there said, "First of all, we have only one date open, and that is June 28."

I said, "Really. That's the only day I want." Because normally they are booked one to two years in advance. But they have a very strict rule that no outside food or drinks are permitted, you have to get it there from their own chef. That's the way they make their money. So that was a bit of a dilemma. But we started brainstorming to see what kind of vegetarian food we could get from them that would meet our standards. Then we gave them a big list of the restrictions and standards we wanted, and the lady said she would give it to their chef. After two weeks we still did not hear from them, so we called and she said, "You know what? This is a very complicated affair. Why don't you do whatever you want. Because we cannot accommodate your request, we allow you to do what you need to do."

I said, "That's what we have been asking."

The next fear was how many people would come to the presentation. We wanted to have a decent turnout for the event, and that is what I was deliberating over when I was in front of my Deities. So I also have a photo of Srila Prabhupada in my temple room, and while I was discussing this with my Gaura Nitai Deities, the garland from Srila Prabhupada's photo fell from it, which it had never done before. So I took that as a sign of blessings and that now we did not have anything to worry about. In the end, everything came together very nicely, from having the date we wanted, being able to bring our own food, which they never allow, and then having a good turnout for the attendance of the event, including the mayor of the town. It was very successful. The Deities fulfilled all our requests.

LORD JAGANNATHA WANTS WATERMELON

As told by Inna. It was a really hot day, July 19, 2011. I was going home from work, and on the way home I stopped to buy groceries for my Lord Jagannatha Deity. For some reason, I kept thinking that Lord Jagannatha wanted a watermelon in this hot temperature. So I picked a big one for Him. When I got home, I felt too tired from work and from being outside, so I put the groceries in the refrigerator and put the watermelon on the kitchen counter. Right after that I entered Lord Jagannatha's room, paid obeisances and said: "Dear Lord Jagannath, if You could please forgive me, I feel so exhausted and need some rest. Let me please have some rest and then I will go to the kitchen and make my offerings to You."

After saying these words, I went to my office, set at my home computer and began going through my unread emails and watching some news. I do this when I feel tired and can't concentrate on anything else. However, as I sat there, I kept feeling guilty that Jagannatha was waiting for me, like He wanted the watermelon. About a half-an-hour later I heard this sudden noise as if something was hit. The sound came from the kitchen. So I rushed to the door to find nobody and nothing there. I began looking around until my glance fell on the watermelon on the counter. The watermelon was cracked in half, and produced a great scent of a red-ripe watermelon! Immediately, I realized what happened and said, "Oh, My Lord Jagannatha, please forgive me, I will bring it to You right away!" I rushed to the back yard, picked two tulasi leaves, detached the two halves of the watermelon, and put one Tulasi leaf on each half. While doing all this I kept talking to my Jagannatha and laughing at the entire situation. Carrying half of the watermelon in each hand, I entered the altar room to put this on the offering table. Much to my delight and amazement, when I looked at the Deities, all Three of Them were laughing! It was so obvious! And, as I was pronouncing the mantras to offer the watermelon to Them, I kept laughing. I even thought that my Deities of Krishna and Narasimhadeva also laughed.

CONCLUSION

So herein I have provided the relevant explanations on the authority and antiquity and importance of Deity worship in the Vedic tradition, and for a person's spiritual development and for attaining a stronger connection with the Divine. I have also presented various stories of people's experiences, both old and recent, which show the unique and multiple ways Krishna will reveal Himself through the Deity forms. There are many more stories that could be used, and new experiences between the Deity and His devotees are happening all the time. But, as previously explained, this shows how Krishna reciprocates or engages in pastimes with people in many ways and at all times, and is not merely a stone image, but acts as He likes and when He likes in personal ways.

The Deity is also a manifestation of the Lord's causeless mercy on all the conditioned souls, or even those devotees who are trying to develop deeper levels of appreciation, love and devotion for the Lord. Thus, the Deity can also give evidence of the reality of the Supreme's existence in the spiritual dimension, the same dimension to which we all naturally belong.

Of course, it takes a certain level of spirituality, in most cases, to perceive this, without which our consciousness is far away from the spiritual plane of existence. What I mean by that is explained in the following verse from the *Padma Purana*:

arcye vishnua shila-dhir gurushu nara-matir vaishnave jati-buddhir vishnor va vaishnavanam kali-mala-mathane pada-tirthe 'mbu-buddhihi

shri-vishnor namni mantre sakala-kalushahe shabda-samanya-buddhir vishnau sarveshvareshe tad itara-samadhir yasya va naraki shah

This verse essentially means that "Persons who consider the Deity of the Supreme Lord to be dead matter, made out of wood, stone or metal, or the spiritual master, who is an eternal associate of the Supreme Lord, to be an ordinary man who is prone to die, or the

Vaishnava to be coming from some caste, or the water that washes the feet of the pure devotee or the Supreme Lord [or His Deity] to be ordinary water, although such water has the potency to destroy all the evils of the age of Kali, or considers the holy name of the Supreme Lord or mantras dedicated to Him, which are able to destroy all sins, to be ordinary sounds, or thinks the Supreme Lord of all, Lord Vishnu, to be on the same level as the demigods, is considered to possess a hellish mentality. A person who thinks in this way is certainly a resident of hell."

This means that a person who lacks the proper understanding about the spiritual nature of the Deity simply lives in an ephemeral world full of temporary forms and elusive ideas that occupy his mind with no ultimate conclusion or solution. But by understanding the spiritual characteristics of the Deity and those who are connected with the Divine in this way, ultimately reach the goal of life.

On a personal level, I have also had numerous experiences with the Deities. I have been a *pujari* (priest) and in close contact with Deities and caring or worshiping Them for many years. I often consult with the Deities for answers to questions or guidance in various situations or projects, or simply for blessings. And many times I have received answers I needed, sometimes immediately and directly as telepathic messages, and other times later in other ways.

For example, once I was in Vrindavana at the Krishna-Balarama Mandir during the evening *arati* and standing in the back of the crowd, just chanting *japa* and looking at the Deities as I often do while there. I was feeling that I should give up on a certain project I had been thinking about, which would take a long time to develop and much thought and energy. It would just be easier not to start it. Then, suddenly, I got a telepathic message that went something like, "How dare you think of quitting! How do you think anything will change if you quit?"

This was a message that came directly from the Deity of Lord Krishna. I was shocked at the directness of it. But it was all I needed to hear to understand that obviously Lord Krishna has a plan and that I was a part of it, and though I'm still not sure exactly how it will manifest, I should continue to work on it and help be the catalyst for it. Once I heard that message, I did not need any further instruction to know what Krishna expected of me and what I was supposed to do. Everything instantly became very clear. This was just one of many such circumstances that has happened to me.

Another time was during my stay in Chicago back in 1978. I had gotten married to Chintamani devi dasi and was greatly attracted to her little Jagannatha Deities. I had great fun in purchasing items for increasing the opulences of Little Lord Jagannatha. Chintamani and I took pleasure in taking turns dressing the Deities, after she had trained me how to do it. And I liked buying beads and crystals to make more necklaces and belts for Their Lordships. I really was focused on keeping everything neat and organized. One time I went on a marathon for six weeks of making all kinds of beaded belts and necklaces for the Deities. I was in a world of my own, and greatly ecstatic. With all that happened in Chicago, the Deities' paraphernalia, which had been rather minimal up to then, easily doubled or tripled during that time.

Various spiritual pastimes continued to happen with Little Lord Jagannatha. One time I was doing the evening *arati* at the Krishna temple where I was serving and Chintamani came down from the upstairs women's *ashrama* to see her Little Lord Jagannatha Deities before going to cook the milksweets. Her Jagannatha Deities were on the main alter in the temple room at the time. I happened to learn that someone else was already cooking the milksweets that evening when I had gone to get the offering from the kitchen to offer to the Deities before doing the *arati*. I thought that if she found someone else cooking them she might get upset. So when I was offering the *arati* in front of Little Lord Jagannatha, I felt I really wanted to tell her about it but couldn't because I couldn't stop the *arati*. Later she told me that when she was standing there, she had received a telepathic message from Little Lord Jagannatha that she wouldn't have to cook the milksweets, and then when she went up to the kitchen she indeed saw that someone else was already doing them. So somehow Little Lord Jagannatha had fulfilled my desire to convey to her the message. These kinds of incidents were always happening from time to time with these Little Lord Jagannatha Deities.

Another time that was quite noteworthy for me was when I was in Dwaraka. I had gone there on one of my typical photographic pilgrimages, and wanted to spend several days there. I had gone to the temple for *darshan* early one day, but it had been quite crowded, so I did what I could at the time to see as much as possible, but I could not get very close for a good view. Then one evening *arati* that I attended was not so crowded and I was able to get to the very front to watch the ceremony. The temple assistant saw me and gave me lots of offered sugar sweets and *tulasi* leaves. I was very surprised at this and felt that this was special mercy from the Lord. As I stood there and watched, I became very ecstatic. Soon it was as if I was seeing nothing else but the Deity. My whole consciousness was focused strictly on the Deity of Lord Dwarakadish. In fact, I could not take my eyes off Him. It became a very powerful *darshan* and meditation in which I felt I was not only looking at Lord Dwarakadish, but He was also looking at and seeing me. I had not experienced such an exchange in a long time. It was very moving and the feeling and energy I got from it made me feel like I was literally floating for days. I was in a different consciousness that made me feel I was no longer merely wandering on this planet earth, but I would walk around town and see other temples while feeling I was in the spiritual realm. That is a taste and experience that you do not forget.

When I started thinking about writing this book I thought I would not include any of my own experiences, but simply focus on what I have heard and learned from others. But now I have broken that idea and have also included a few of my own stories and experiences. But this is possible for anyone. It is all up to Lord Krishna and the other Divinities as to who They offer their blessings. You simply have to be open to it, especially with love. There is another world out there, all around us. And this is one of the ways in which that spiritual dimension can open up for us. I take great pleasure in explaining and relating these stories that show the glories, potency and causeless mercy of the Lord in this way.

GLOSSARY

Acarya--the spiritual master who sets the proper standard by his own example.

Advaita--nondual, meaning that the Absolute Truth is one, and that there is no individuality between the Supreme Being and the individual souls which merge into oneness, the Brahman, when released from material existence. The philosophy taught by Sankaracharya.

Agni--fire, or Agni the demigod of fire.

Agnihotra--the Vedic sacrifice in which offerings were made to the fire, such as ghee, milk, sesame seeds, grains, etc. The demigod Agni would deliver the offerings to the demigods that are referred to in the ritual.

Ahimsa--nonviolence.

Akarma--actions which cause no *karmic* reactions.

Ananda--spiritual bliss.

Ananta--unlimited.

Arati--the ceremony of worship when incense and ghee lamps are offered to the Deities.

Arca-vigraha--the worshipable Deity form of the Lord made of stone, wood, etc.

Asana--postures for meditation, or exercises for developing the body into a fit instrument for spiritual advancement.

Asat--that which is temporary.

Ashrama--one of the four orders of spiritual life, such as *brahmacari* (celibate student), *grihastha* (married householder), *vanaprastha* (retired stage), and *sannyasa* (renunciate); or the abode of a spiritual teacher or *sadhu*.

Ashvamedha--a Vedic ritual involving offerings to God made by brahmana priests.

Atma--the self or soul. Sometimes means the body, mind, and senses.

Atman--usually referred to as the Supreme Self.

Avatara--an incarnation of the Lord who descends from the spiritual world.

Aum--*om* or *pranava*

Ayurveda--the original wholistic form of medicine as described in the Vedic literature.

168

Badrinatha--one of the holy places of pilgrimage in the Himalayas, and home of the Deity Sri Badrinatha along with many sages and hermits.

Bhagavan--one who possesses all opulences, God.

Bhajan--song of worship.

Bhajan kutir--a small dwelling used for one's worship and meditation.

Bhakta--a devotee of the Lord who is engaged in *bhakti-yoga*.

Bhakti--love and devotion for God.

Bhakti-yoga--the path of offering pure devotional service to the Supreme.

Bhava--preliminary stage of love of God.

Brahmacari--a celebate student, usually five to twenty-five years of age, who is trained by the spiritual master. One of the four divisions or *ashramas* of spiritual life.

Brahmajyoti--the great white light or effulgence which emanates from the body of the Lord.

Brahmaloka--the highest planet or plane of existence in the universe; the planet where Lord Brahma lives.

Brahman--the spiritual energy; the all-pervading impersonal aspect of the Lord; or the Supreme Lord Himself.

Brahmana or brahmin--one of the four orders of society; the intellectual class of men who have been trained in the knowledge of the *Vedas* and initiated by a spiritual master.

Brahminical--to be clean and upstanding, both outwardly and inwardly, like a *brahmana* should be.

Caitanya-caritamrta--the scripture by Krishnadasa Kaviraja which explains the teachings and pastimes of Lord Chaitanya Mahaprabhu.

Caranamrita--the water that has been used to bathe the Deity and is offered in small spoonfuls to visitors in the temple.

Chaitanya Mahaprabhu--the most recent incarnation of the Lord who appeared in the 15th century in Bengal and who originally started the *sankirtana* movement, based on congregational chanting of the holy names.

Chakra--a wheel, disk, or psychic energy center situated along the spinal column in the subtle body of the physical shell.

Cit or *chit*--eternal knowledge.

Darshan--the devotional act of seeing and being seen by the Deity in the temple.

Dashavatara--the ten incarnations of Lord Vishnu: Matsya, Kurma, Varaha, Narasimha, Vamana, Parashurama, Rama, Krishna, Buddha, and Kalki.

Deity--the *arca-vigraha*, or worshipful form of the Divinity in the temple.

Deva–a demigod, or higher being.

Devaloka--the higher planets or planes of existence of the devas.

Devas--demigods or heavenly beings from higher levels of material existence, or a godly person.

Dham--a holy place.

Dharma--the essential nature or duty of the living being.

Dharmachakra--Buddhist wheel of law, the first sermon given by Buddha at Sarnath.

Diksha--spiritual initiation.

Divya Desam–One of the 108 most important Vishnu temples in India.

Diwali--festival of lights, marks the end of the rainy season.

Dualism--as related in this book, it refers to the Supreme as both an impersonal force (Brahman) as well as the Supreme Person.

Dwaita--dualism, the principle that the Absolute Truth consists of the infinite Supreme Being along with the infinitesimal, individual souls.

Ganesh--a son of Shiva, said to destroy obstacles (as Vinayaka) and offer good luck to those who petition him. It is generally accepted that the way Ganesh got the head of an elephant is that one time Parvati asked him to guard her residence. When Shiva wanted to enter, Ganesh stopped him, which made Shiva very angry. Not recognizing Ganesh, Shiva chopped off his head, which was then destroyed by one of Shiva's goblin associates. Parvati was so upset when she learned what had happened, Shiva, not being able to find Ganesh's original head, took the head of the first creature he saw, which was an elephant, and put it on the body of Ganesh and brought him back to life. The large mouse carrier of Ganesh symbolizes Ganesh's ability to destroy all obstacles, as rodents can gradually gnaw their way through most anything.

Gangapuja--the *arati* ceremony for worshiping the Ganges.

Ganges--the sacred and spiritual river which, according to the *Vedas*, runs throughout the universe, a portion of which is seen in India. The reason the river is considered holy is that it is said to be a drop of the Karana Ocean outside of the universe that leaked in when Lord Vishnu, in His incarnation as Gaudiya--a part of India sometimes called

Aryavarta or land of the Aryans, located south of the Himalayas and north of the Vindhya Hills.

Gaudiya *sampradaya*--the school of Vaishnavism founded by Sri Caitanya.

Gayatri--the spiritual vibration or *mantra* from which the other *Vedas* were expanded and which is chanted by those who are initiated as *brahmanas* and given the spiritual understanding of Vedic philosophy.

Goloka Vrindavana--the name of Lord Krishna's spiritual planet.

Gompa--Buddhist monastery.

Gopuram--the tall ornate towers that mark the gates to the temples, often found in south India.

Gosvami--one who is master of the senses.

Govardhana-shila–a sacred stone from Govardhana Hill, considered as a direct form or expansion of Lord Krishna.

Govinda--a name of Krishna which means one who gives pleasure to the cows and senses.

Govindaraja--Krishna as Lord of the Cowherds.

Grihastha--the householder order of life. One of the four *ashramas* in spiritual life.

Guru--a spiritual master.

Hanuman--the popular monkey servant of Lord Rama.

Hare--the Lord's pleasure potency, Radharani, who is approached for accessibility to the Lord.

Hari--a name of Krishna as the one who takes away one's obstacles on the spiritual path.

Haribol--a word that means to chant the name of the Lord, Hari.

Harinam--refers to the name of the Lord, Hari.

Impersonalism--the view that God has no personality or form, but is only an impersonal force (Brahman) which the individual souls merge back into when released from material existence.

Impersonalist--those who believe God has no personality or form.

Incarnation--the taking on of a body or form.

Jagannatha----Krishna as Lord of the Universe, especially as worshipped in Jagannatha Puri.

Jai or *Jaya*--a term meaning victory, all glories.

Japa--the chanting one performs, usually softly, for one's own meditation.

Jyotirlinga--the luminous energy of Shiva manifested as a self-manifested *lingam* at one of 12 places, such as Kedarnatha, Patan, Ujjain, and Varanasi.

Kali-yuga--the fourth and present age, the age of quarrel and confusion, which lasts 432,000 years and began 5,000 years ago.

Kalki--future incarnation of Lord Vishnu who appears at the end of Kali-yuga.

Karma--material actions performed in regard to developing one's position or for future results which produce *karmic* reactions. It is also the reactions one endures from such fruitive activities.

Karma-kanda--the portion of the *Vedas* which primarily deals with recommended fruitive activities for various results.

Karma-yoga--system of yoga for using one's activities for spiritual advancement.

Karmi--the fruitive worker, one who accumulates more *karma*.

Keshava--Krishna with long hair.

Kirtana--chanting or singing the glories of the Lord.

Krishna--the name of the original Supreme Personality of Godhead which means the most attractive and greatest pleasure. He is the source of all other incarnations, such as Vishnu, Rama, Narasimha, Narayana, Buddha, Parashurama, Vamanadeva, Kalki at the end of Kali-yuga, etc.

Krishnaloka--the spiritual planet where Lord Krishna resides.

Kshatriya--the second class of *varna* of society, or occupation of administrative or protective service, such as warrior or military personel.

Ksirodakasayi Vishnu--the Supersoul expansion of the Lord who enters into each atom and the heart of each individual.

Kumbha Mela--the holy festival in which millions of pilgrims and sages gather to bathe in the holy and purifying rivers for liberation at particular auspicious times that are calculated astrologically. The Kumbha Mela festivals take place every three years alternating between Allahabad, Nasik, Ujjain, and Hardwar.

Kuruksetra--the place of battle 5,000 years ago between the Pandavas and the Lakshmi--the goddess of fortune and wife of Lord Vishnu.

Lila--pastimes.

Lilavataras--the many incarnations of God who appear to display various spiritual pastimes to attract the conditioned souls in the material world.

Madana-mohana--name of Krishna as one who fills the mind with love.

Mahabharata--the great epic of the Pandavas, which includes the *Bhagavad-gita*, by Vyasadeva.

Maha-mantra--the best *mantra* for self-realization in this age, called the Hare Krishna *mantra*.

Maha-Vishnu or Karanodakasayi Vishnu--the Vishnu expansion of Lord Krishna from whom all the material universes emanate.

Mandir--a temple.

Mantra--a sound vibration which prepares the mind for spiritual realization and delivers the mind from material inclinations. In some cases a *mantra* is chanted for specific material benefits.

Maya--illusion, or anything that appears to not be connected with the eternal Absolute Truth.

Moksha--liberation from material existence.

Murti--a Deity of the Lord or an image of a demigod or spiritual master that is worshiped.

Narasimha--Lord Vishnu's incarnation as the half-man half-lion who killed the demon Hiranyakashipu.

Narayana--the four-handed form of the Supreme Lord.

Nityananda–the brother of Sri Chaitanya, and *avatara* of Lord Balarama.

Om or *Omkara*--*pranava*, the transcendental *om mantra*, generally referring to the attributeless or impersonal aspects of the Absolute.

Paramatma--the Supersoul, or localized expansion of the Lord.

Parampara--the system of disciplic succession through which transcendental knowledge descends.

Parthasarathi--Krishna as Arjuna's chariot driver.

Prana--the life air or cosmic energy.

Pranayama--control of the breathing process as in *astanga* or *raja-yoga*.

Pranava--same as *omkara*.

Prasada--food or other articles that have been offered to the Deity in the temple and then distributed amongst people as the blessings or mercy of the Deity.

Prema--matured love for Krishna.

Puja--the worship offered to the Deity.

Pujari--the priest who performs worship, *puja*, to the Deity.

Radha--Krishna's favorite devotee and the personification of His bliss potency.

Ramachandra--an incarnation of Krishna as He appeared as the greatest of kings.

Ramanuja--Vaishnava philosopher.

Ramayana--the great epic of the incarnation of Lord Ramachandra.

Rasa--an enjoyable taste or feeling, a relationship with God.

Ravana--demon king of the *Ramayana*.

Rishi--saintly person who knows the Vedic knowledge.

Sac-cid-ananda-vigraha--the transcendental form of the Lord or of the living entity which is eternal, full of knowledge and bliss.

Sadhana--a specific practice or discipline for attaining God realization.

Sadhu--Indian holy man or devotee.

Samadhi--trance, the perfection of being absorbed in the Absolute.

Samsara--rounds of life; cycles of birth and death; reincarnation.

Sanatana-dharma--the eternal nature of the living being, to love and render service to the supreme lovable object, the Lord.

Sankirtana-yajna–the prescribed sacrifice for this age: congregational chanting of the holy names of God.

Sannyasa--the renounced order of life, the highest of the four *ashramas* on the spiritual path.

Satya-yuga--the first of the four ages which lasts 1,728,000 years.

Shabda-brahma--the original spiritual vibration or energy of which the *Vedas* are composed.

Shalagrama-shila–the sacred stone that is accepted as a direct form of Lord Vishnu.

Shastra--the authentic revealed Vedic scripture.

Shiva--the benevolent one, the demigod who is in charge of the material mode of ignorance and the destruction of the universe. Part of the triad of Brahma, Vishnu, and Shiva who continually create, maintain, and destroy the universe. He is known as Rudra when displaying his destructive aspect.

Sikha--a tuft of hair on the back of the head signifying that one is a Vaishnava.

Sravanam--hearing about the Lord.

Srimad-Bhagavatam--the most ripened fruit of the tree of Vedic knowledge compiled by Vyasadeva.

Sruti--scriptures that were received directly from God and transmitted orally by *brahmanas* or *rishis* down through succeeding generations. Traditionally, it is considered the four primary *Vedas*.

Sudra--the working class of society, the fourth of the *varnas*.

Surya--Sun or solar deity.

Svami--one who can control his mind and senses.

Tilok--the clay markings that signify a person's body as a temple, and the sect or school of thought of the person.

Tirtha--a holy place of pilgrimage.

Treta-yuga--the second of the four ages which lasts 1,296,000 years.

Trivikrama--Lord Vishnu as Vamadeva, the *brahmana* dwarf who covered the entire universe in three steps.

Tulasi--the small tree that grows where worship to Krishna is found. It is called the embodiment of devotion, and the incarnation of Vrinda-devi.

Upanishads--the portions of the *Vedas* which primarily explain philosophically the Absolute Truth. It is knowledge of Brahman which releases one from the world and allows one to attain self-realization when received from a qualified teacher. Except for the *Isa Upanishad*, which is the 40th chapter of the *Vaikunthas*--the planets located in the spiritual sky.

Vaishnava--a worshiper of the Supreme Lord Vishnu or Krishna and His expansions or incarnations.

Vaishnava-*aparadha*--an offense against a Vaisnava or devotee, which can negate all of one's spiritual progress.

Vaisya--the third class of society engaged in business or farming.

Varaha--Lord Vishnu's boar incarnation.

Varna--sometimes referred to as caste, a division of society, such as *brahmana* (a priestly intellectual), a *kshatriya* (ruler or manager), *vaisya* (a merchant, banker, or farmer), and *sudra* (common laborer).

Varnashrama--the system of four divisions of society and four orders of spiritual life.

Vasudeva--Krishna.

Vedanta-sutras--the philosophical conclusion of the four *Vedas*.

Vedas--generally means the four primary *samhitas; Rig, Yajur, Sama, Atharva.*

Venktateshvara--Vishnu as Lord of the Venkata Hills, worshiped in Tirumala.

Vishnu--the expansion of Lord Krishna who enters into the material energy to create and maintain the cosmic world.

Vishvakarma--demigod architect of the heavens.

Vrindavana--the place where Lord Krishna displayed His village pastimes 5,000 years ago, and is considered to be part of the spiritual abode.

Yamuna--goddess personification of the Yamuna River.

Yashoda--foster mother of Krishna.

Yatra--a pilgrimage to the holy places.

Yuga-avataras--the incarnations of God who appear in each of the four *yugas* to explain the authorized system of self-realization in that age.

REFERENCES

Art of Sadhana: A Guide to Daily Devotion, by Swami B. P. Puri Maharaja, Mandala Publishing Group, San Francisco, CA.

Bhagavad-gita As It Is, translated by A. C. Bhaktivedanta Swami, Bhaktivedanta Book Trust, New York/Los Angeles, 1972

Bhakti-rasamrita-sindhu, (Nectar of Devotion), translated by A. C. Bhaktivedanta Swami, Bhaktivedanta Book Trust, New York/Los Angeles, 1970

Bhakti Rasamarita Sindhu, by Srila Rupa Gosvami, trans. By Bhanu Swami, Sri Vaikuntha Enterprises, Chennai, 2003

Caitanya-caritamrta, translated by A. C. Bhaktivedanta Swami, Bhaktivedanta Book Trust, Los Angeles, 1974

Darshan, Seeing the Divine Image in India, Diana Eck, Anima Books, Chambersberg, PA, 1985

Experience in Bhakti: The Science Celestial, by Dr. O. B. L. Kapoor, Published by Sri Badrinarayana Bhagavata Bhushana Prabhu, 1994.

Gopal-tapani Upanishad, by Krsna Dvaipayana Vedavyasa, commentary by Visvanatha Cakravarti Thakura, translated by Bhumipati dasa, Ras Bihari Lal & Sons, Loi Bazaar, Vrindaban, UP, 281121, India, 2004

The Gosvamis of Vrindavana, O.B.L.Kapoor, Sarasvati Jayasri Classics, Delhi, 1994

The Hidden Treasure of the Holy Dham Nabadvipa, Srila Bhaktivinoda Thakura, Ananta Printing and Publishing and Mandala Media Group, Soquel, CA, 1993

The Lilas of Lord Jagannatha, by Somanath Khuntia, Vedic Cultural Association, 1990.

Pastimes and History of Lord Jagannatha in Rajapur, by Pankajanghri Dasa, Gauranga Releases, Scotland, 2007

Seeing Spiritual India, by Stephen Knapp

Sri Jagannatha: The Pastimes of the Lord of the Universe, by Bhakti Purusottama Swami, Bhaktivedanta Book Trust, Sri Mayapur Dham, India, 2006

Srimad-Bhagavatam, translated by A. C. Bhaktivedanta Swami, Bhaktivedanta Book trust, New York/Los Angeles, 1972

Story of Rasikananda, Gopijanavallabha dasa, edited by Bhakti Vikas Swami, Mumbai, 1997

INDEX

ABOUT THE AUTHOR

Stephen Knapp grew up in a Christian family, during which time he seriously studied the Bible to understand its teachings. In his late teenage years, however, he sought answers to questions not easily explained in Christian theology. So he began to search through other religions and philosophies from around the world and started to find the answers for which he was looking. He also studied a variety of occult sciences, ancient mythology, mysticism, yoga, and the spiritual teachings of the East. After his first reading of the *Bhagavad-gita*, he felt he had found the last piece of the puzzle he had been putting together through all of his research. Therefore, he continued to study all of the major Vedic texts of India to gain a better understanding of the Vedic science.

It is known amongst all Eastern mystics that anyone, regardless of qualifications, academic or otherwise, who does not engage in the spiritual practices described in the Vedic texts cannot actually enter into understanding the depths of the Vedic spiritual science, nor acquire the realizations that should accompany it. So, rather than pursuing his research in an academic atmosphere at a university, Stephen directly engaged in the spiritual disciplines that have been recommended for hundreds of years. He continued his study of Vedic knowledge and spiritual practice under the guidance of a spiritual master. Through this process, and with the sanction of His Divine Grace A. C. Bhaktivedanta Swami Prabhupada, he became initiated into the genuine and authorized spiritual line of the Brahma-Madhava-Gaudiya *sampradaya*, which is a disciplic succession that descends back through Sri Caitanya Mahaprabhu and Sri Vyasadeva, the compiler of Vedic literature, and further back to Sri Krishna. Besides being *brahminically* initiated, Stephen has also been to India several times and traveled extensively throughout the country, visiting most of the major holy places and gaining a wide variety of spiritual experiences that only such places can give.

Stephen has put the culmination of over forty years of continuous research and travel experience into his books in an effort to share it with those who are also looking for spiritual understanding. More books are forthcoming, so stay in touch through his website to find out further developments.

More information about Stephen, his projects, books, free ebooks, and numerous articles and videos can be found on his website at: www.stephen-knapp.com or at http://stephenknapp.wordpress.com.

Stephen has continued to write books that include in *The Eastern Answers ot the Mysteries of Life* series:
The Secret Teachings of the Vedas,
The Universal Path to Enlightenment,
The Vedic Prophecies: A New Look into the Future,
How the Universe was Created and Our Purpose In It.
He has also written:
Toward World Peace: Seeing the Unity Between Us All,
Facing Death: Welcoming the Afterlife,
The Key to Real Happiness,
Proof of Vedic Culture's Global Existence,
Vedic Culture: The Difference It Can Make In Your Life,
Reincarnation and Karma: How They Really Affect Us,
Power of the Dharma: An Introduction to Hinduism and Vedic Culture,
The Eleventh Commandment: The Next Step in Social Spiritual Development,
The Heart of Hinduism: The Eastern Path to Freedom, Empowerment and Illumination,
Seeing Spiritual India: A Guide to Temples, Holy Sites, Festivals and Traditions,
Crimes Against India: And the Need to Protect its Vedic Tradition,
Avatars, Gods and Goddesses of the Vedic Tradition,
The Soul: Understanding Our Real Identity,
Prayers, Mantras and Gayatris: A Collection for Insight, Protection, Spiritual Growth, and Many Other Blessings, and
Destined for Infinity, an exciting novel for those who prefer lighter reading, or learning spiritual knowledge in the context of an action oriented, spiritual adventure.

If you have enjoyed this book, or if you are serious about finding higher levels of real spiritual Truth, and learning more about the mysteries of India's Vedic culture, then you will also want to get other books written by Stephen Knapp, which include:

The Secret Teachings of the Vedas

The Eastern Answers to the Mysteries of Life

This book presents the essence of the ancient Eastern philosophy and summarizes some of the most elevated and important of all spiritual knowledge. This enlightening information is explained in a clear and concise way and is essential for all who want to increase their spiritual understanding, regardless of what their religious background may be. If you are looking for a book to give you an in-depth introduction to the Vedic spiritual knowledge, and to get you started in real spiritual understanding, this is the book!

The topics include: What is your real spiritual identity; the Vedic explanation of the soul; scientific evidence that consciousness is separate from but interacts with the body; the real unity between us all; how to attain the highest happiness and freedom from the cause of suffering; the law of karma and reincarnation; the karma of a nation; where you are really going in life; the real process of progressive evolution; life after death—heaven, hell, or beyond; a description of the spiritual realm; the nature of the Absolute Truth—personal God or impersonal force; recognizing the existence of the Supreme; the reason why we exist at all; and much more. This book provides the answers to questions not found in other religions or philosophies, and condenses information from a wide variety of sources that would take a person years to assemble. It also contains many quotations from the Vedic texts to let the texts speak for themselves, and to show the knowledge the Vedas have held for thousands of years. It also explains the history and origins of the Vedic literature. This book has been called one of the best reviews of Eastern philosophy available.

The Universal Path to Enlightenment
The Way to Spiritual Success for Everyone

Although all religions and spiritual processes are meant to lead you toward enlightenment, they are not all the same in regard to the methods they teach, nor in the level of philosophical understanding they offer. So an intelligent person will make comparisons between them to understand the aims and distinctions of each religion, and which is the most elevating.

This book presents a most interesting and revealing survey of the major spiritual paths of the world and describes their histories, philosophical basis, and goals. It will help you decide which path may be the best for you.

You Will Learn

- the essential similarities of all religions that all people of any culture or tradition can practice, which could bring about a united world religion, or "THE UNIVERSAL PATH TO ENLIGHTENMENT."
- how Christianity and Judaism were greatly influenced by the early pre-Christian or "pagan" religions and adopted many of their legends, holidays, and rituals that are still accepted and practiced today.
- about evidence that shows Jesus traveled to India to learn its spiritual knowledge, and then made bhakti-yoga the basis of his teachings.
- the philosophical basis and origin of Christianity, Judaism, Islam, Hinduism, Buddhism, Zoroastrianism, Jainism, Sikhism, and many others.
- and, most importantly, what is the real purpose that you should strive for in a spiritual process, and how to practice the path that is especially recommended as the easiest and most effective for the people of this age.

This book is $19.95, 6"x9" trim size, 340 pages, ISBN: 1453644660.

The Vedic Prophecies:
A New Look into the Future

The Vedic prophecies take you to the end of time! This is the first book ever to present the unique predictions found in the ancient Vedic texts of India. These prophecies are like no others and will provide you with a very different view of the future and how things fit together in the plan for the universe.

Now you can discover the amazing secrets that are hidden in the oldest spiritual writings on the planet. Find out what they say about the distant future, and what the seers of long ago saw in their visions of the destiny of the world.

This book will reveal predictions of deteriorating social changes and how to avoid them; future droughts and famines; low-class rulers and evil governments; whether there will be another appearance (second coming) of God; and predictions of a new spiritual awareness and how it will spread around the world. You will also learn the answers to such questions as:

- Does the future get worse or better?
- Will there be future world wars or global disasters?
- What lies beyond the predictions of Nostradamus, the Mayan prophecies, or the Biblical apocalypse?
- Are we in the end times? How to recognize them if we are.
- Does the world come to an end? If so, when and how?

Now you can find out what the future holds. The Vedic Prophecies carry an important message and warning for all humanity, which needs to be understood now!

Order your copy: ISBN: 1461002249, $20.95, 328 pages.

How the Universe was Created And Our Purpose In It

This book provides answers and details about the process of creation that are not available in any other traditions, religions, or areas of science. It offers the oldest rendition of the creation and presents insights into the spiritual purpose of it and what we are really meant to do here.

Every culture in the world and most religions have their own descriptions of the creation, and ideas about from where we came and what we should do. Unfortunately, these are often short and generalized versions that lack details. Thus, they are often given no better regard than myths. However, there are descriptions that give more elaborate explanations of how the cosmic creation fully manifested which are found in the ancient Vedic *Puranas* of India, some of the oldest spiritual writings on the planet. These descriptions provide the details and answers that other versions leave out. Furthermore, these Vedic descriptions often agree, and sometimes disagree, with the modern scientific theories of creation, and offer some factors that science has yet to consider.

Now, with this book, we can get a clearer understanding of how this universe appears, what is its real purpose, from where we really came, how we fit into the plan for the universe, and if there is a way out of here. Some of the many topics included are:

Comparisons between other creation legends.

Detailed descriptions of the dawn of creation and how the material energy developed and caused the formation of the cosmos.

What is the primary source of the material and spiritual elements.

Insights into the primal questions of, "Who am I? Why am I here? Where have I come from? What is the purpose of this universe and my life?"

An alternative description of the evolutionary development of the various forms of life.

Seeing beyond the temporary nature of the material worlds, and more.

This book will provide some of the most profound insights into these questions and topics. It will also give any theist more information and understanding about how the universe is indeed a creation of God.

This book is $19.95, 6" x 9" trim size, 308 pages, ISBN: 1456460455.

Proof of Vedic Culture's Global Existence

This book provides evidence which makes it clear that the ancient Vedic culture was once a global society. Even today we can see its influence in any part of the world. Thus, it becomes obvious that before the world became full of distinct and separate cultures, religions and countries, it was once united in a common brotherhood of Vedic culture, with common standards, principles, and representations of God.

No matter what we may consider our present religion, society or country, we are all descendants of this ancient global civilization. Thus, the Vedic culture is the parent of all humanity and the original ancestor of all religions. In this way, we all share a common heritage.

This book is an attempt to allow humanity to see more clearly its universal roots. This book provides a look into:

- How Vedic knowledge was given to humanity by the Supreme.
- The history and traditional source of the Vedas and Vedic Aryan society.
- Who were the original Vedic Aryans. How Vedic society was a global influence and what shattered this world-wide society. How Sanskrit faded from being a global language.
- Many scientific discoveries over the past several centuries are only rediscoveries of what the Vedic literature already knew.
- How the origins of world literature are found in India and Sanskrit.
- The links between the Vedic and other ancient cultures, such as the Sumerians, Persians, Egyptians, Romans, Greeks, and others.
- Links between the Vedic tradition and Judaism, Christianity, Islam, and Buddhism.
- How many of the western holy sites, churches, and mosques were once the sites of Vedic holy places and sacred shrines.
- The Vedic influence presently found in such countries as Britain, France, Russia, Greece, Israel, Arabia, China, Japan, and in areas of Scandinavia, the Middle East, Africa, the South Pacific, and the Americas.
- Uncovering the truth of India's history: Powerful evidence that shows how many mosques and Muslim buildings were once opulent Vedic temples, including the Taj Mahal, Delhi's Jama Masjid, Kutab Minar, as well as buildings in many other cities, such as Agra, Ahmedabad, Bijapur, etc.
- How there is presently a need to plan for the survival of Vedic culture.

This book is sure to provide some amazing facts and evidence about the truth of world history and the ancient, global Vedic Culture. This book has enough startling information and historical evidence to cause a major shift in the way we view religious history and the basis of world traditions.

This book is $20.99, 6"x9" trim size, 431 pages, ISBN: 978-1-4392-4648-1.

Toward World Peace: Seeing the Unity Between Us All

This book points out the essential reasons why peace in the world and cooperation amongst people, communities, and nations have been so difficult to establish. It also advises the only way real peace and harmony amongst humanity can be achieved.

In order for peace and unity to exist we must first realize what barriers and divisions keep us apart. Only then can we break through those barriers to see the unity that naturally exists between us all. Then, rather than focus on our differences, it is easier to recognize our similarities and common goals. With a common goal established, all of humanity can work together to help each other reach that destiny.

This book is short and to the point. It is a thought provoking book and will provide inspiration for anyone. It is especially useful for those working in politics, religion, interfaith, race relations, the media, the United Nations, teaching, or who have a position of leadership in any capacity. It is also for those of us who simply want to spread the insights needed for bringing greater levels of peace, acceptance, unity, and equality between friends, neighbours, and communities. Such insights include:

- The factors that keep us apart.
- Breaking down cultural distinctions.
- Breaking down the religious differences.
- Seeing through bodily distinctions.
- We are all working to attain the same things.
- Our real identity: The basis for common ground.
- Seeing the Divinity within each of us.
- What we can do to bring unity between everyone we meet.

This book carries an important message and plan of action that we must incorporate into our lives and plans for the future if we intend to ever bring peace and unity between us.

This book is $6.95, 90 pages, 6" x 9" trim size, ISBN: 1452813744.

Facing Death
Welcoming the Afterlife

Many people are afraid of death, or do not know how to prepare for it nor what to expect. So this book is provided to relieve anyone of the fear that often accompanies the thought of death, and to supply a means to more clearly understand the purpose of it and how we can use it to our advantage. It will also help the survivors of the departed souls to better understand what has happened and how to cope with it. Furthermore, it shows that death is not a tragedy, but a natural course of events meant to help us reach our destiny.

This book is easy to read, with soothing and comforting wisdom, along with stories of people who have been with departing souls and what they have experienced. It is written especially for those who have given death little thought beforehand, but now would like to have some preparedness for what may need to be done regarding the many levels of the experience and what might take place during this transition.

To assist you in preparing for your own death, or that of a loved one, you will find guidelines for making one's final days as peaceful and as smooth as possible, both physically and spiritually. Preparing for deathcan transform your whole outlook in a positive way, if understood properly. Some of the topics in the book include:

- The fear of death and learning to let go.
- The opportunity of death: The portal into the next life.
- This earth and this body are no one's real home, so death is natural.
- Being practical and dealing with the final responsibilities.
- Forgiving yourself and others before you go.
- Being the assistant of one leaving this life.
- Connecting with the person inside the disease.
- Surviving the death of a loved one.
- Stories of being with dying, and an amazing near-death-experience.
- Connecting to the spiritual side of death.
- What happens while leaving the body.
- What difference the consciousness makes during death, and how to attain the best level of awareness to carry you through it, or what death will be like and how to prepare for it, this book will help you.

Published by iUniverse.com, $13.95, 135 pages, ISBN: 978-1-4401-1344-4

Destined for Infinity

Deep within the mystical and spiritual practices of India are doors that lead to various levels of both higher and lower planes of existence. Few people from the outside are ever able to enter into the depths of these practices to experience such levels of reality.

This is the story of the mystical adventure of a man, Roman West, who entered deep into the secrets of India where few other Westerners have been able to penetrate. While living with a master in the Himalayan foothills and traveling the mystical path that leads to the Infinite, he witnesses the amazing powers the mystics can achieve and undergoes some of the most unusual experiences of his life. Under the guidance of a master that he meets in the mountains, he gradually develops mystic abilities of his own and attains the sacred vision of the enlightened sages and enters the unfathomable realm of Infinity. However, his peaceful life in the hills comes to an abrupt end when he is unexpectedly forced to confront the powerful forces of darkness that have been unleashed by an evil Tantric priest to kill both Roman and his master. His only chance to defeat the intense forces of darkness depends on whatever spiritual strength he has been able to develop.

This story includes traditions and legends that have existed for hundreds and thousands of years. All of the philosophy, rituals, mystic powers, forms of meditation, and descriptions of the Absolute are authentic and taken from narrations found in many of the sacred books of the East, or gathered by the author from his own experiences in India and information from various sages themselves.

This book will will prepare you to perceive the multi-dimensional realities that exist all around us, outside our sense perception. This is a book that will give you many insights into the broad possibilities of our life and purpose in this world.

Published by iUniverse.com, $16.95, 255 pages, 6" x 9" trim size, ISBN: 0-595-33959-X.

Reincarnation and Karma: How They Really Affect Us

Everyone may know a little about reincarnation, but few understand the complexities and how it actually works. Now you can find out how reincarnation and karma really affect us. Herein all of the details are provided on how a person is implicated for better or worse by their own actions. You will understand why particular situations in life happen, and how to make improvements for one's future. You will see why it appears that bad things happen to good people, or even why good things happen to bad people, and what can be done about it.

Other topics include:
- Reincarnation recognized throughout the world
- The most ancient teachings on reincarnation
- Reincarnation in Christianity
- How we transmigrate from one body to another
- Life between lives
- Going to heaven or hell
- The reason for reincarnation
- Free will and choice
- Karma of the nation
- How we determine our own destiny
- What our next life may be like
- Becoming free from all karma and how to prepare to make our next life the best possible.

Combine this with modern research into past life memories and experiences and you will have a complete view of how reincarnation and karma really operate.

Published by iUniverse.com, $13.95, 135 pages, 6" x 9" trim size, ISBN: 0-595-34199-3.

Vedic Culture
The Difference It Can Make In Your Life

The Vedic culture of India is rooted in Sanatana-dharma, the eternal and universal truths that are beneficial to everyone. It includes many avenues of self-development that an increasing number of people from the West are starting to investigate and use, including:

- Yoga
- Meditation and spiritual practice
- Vedic astrology
- Ayurveda
- Vedic gemology
- Vastu or home arrangement
- Environmental awareness
- Vegetarianism
- Social cooperation and arrangement
- The means for global peace
- And much more

Vedic Culture: The Difference It Can Make In Your Life shows the advantages of the Vedic paths of improvement and self-discovery that you can use in your life to attain higher personal awareness, happiness, and fulfillment. It also provides a new view of what these avenues have to offer from some of the most prominent writers on Vedic culture in the West, who discovered how it has affected and benefited their own lives. They write about what it has done for them and then explain how their particular area of interest can assist others. The noted authors include, David Frawley, Subhash Kak, Chakrapani Ullal, Michael Cremo, Jeffrey Armstrong, Robert Talyor, Howard Beckman, Andy Fraenkel, George Vutetakis, Pratichi Mathur, Dhan Rousse, Arun Naik, and Stephen Knapp, all of whom have authored numerous books or articles of their own.

For the benefit of individuals and social progress, the Vedic system is as relevant today as it was in ancient times. Discover why there is a growing renaissance in what the Vedic tradition has to offer in *Vedic Culture*.

Published by iUniverse.com, 300 pages, 6"x 9" trim size, $22.95, ISBN: 0-595-37120-5.

The Heart of Hinduism:
The Eastern Path to Freedom, Empowerment and Illumination

This is a definitive and easy to understand guide to the essential as well as devotional heart of the Vedic/Hindu philosophy. You will see the depths of wisdom and insights that are contained within this profound spiritual knowledge. It is especially good for anyone who lacks the time to research the many topics that are contained within the numerous Vedic manuscripts and to see the advantages of knowing them. This also provides you with a complete process for progressing on the spiritual path, making way for individual empowerment, freedom, and spiritual illumination. All the information is now at your fingertips.

Some of the topics you will find include:
- A complete review of all the Vedic texts and the wide range of topics they contain. This also presents the traditional origins of the Vedic philosophy and how it was developed, and their philosophical conclusion.
- The uniqueness and freedom of the Vedic system.
- A description of the main yoga processes and their effectiveness.
- A review of the Vedic Gods, such as Krishna, Shiva, Durga, Ganesh, and others. You will learn the identity and purpose of each.
- You will have the essential teachings of Lord Krishna who has given some of the most direct and insightful of all spiritual messages known to humanity, and the key to direct spiritual perception.
- The real purpose of yoga and the religious systems.
- What is the most effective spiritual path for this modern age and what it can do for you, with practical instructions for deep realizations.
- The universal path of devotion, the one world religion.
- How Vedic culture is the last bastion of deep spiritual truth.
- Plus many more topics and information for your enlightenment.

So to dive deep into what is Hinduism and the Vedic path to freedom and spiritual perception, this book will give you a jump start. Knowledge is the process of personal empowerment, and no knowledge will give you more power than deep spiritual understanding. And those realizations described in the Vedic culture are the oldest and some of the most profound that humanity has ever known.

Published by iUniverse.com, 650 pages, $35.95, 6" x 9" trim size, ISBN: 0-595-35075-5.

The Power of the Dharma
An Introduction to Hinduism and Vedic Culture

The Power of the Dharma offers you a concise and easy-to-understand overview of the essential principles and customs of Hinduism and the reasons for them. It provides many insights into the depth and value of the timeless wisdom of Vedic spirituality and why the Dharmic path has survived for so many hundreds of years. It reveals why the Dharma is presently enjoying a renaissance of an increasing number of interested people who are exploring its teachings and seeing what its many techniques of Self-discovery have to offer.

Herein you will find:

- Quotes by noteworthy people on the unique qualities of Hinduism
- Essential principles of the Vedic spiritual path
- Particular traits and customs of Hindu worship and explanations of them
- Descriptions of the main Yoga systems
- The significance and legends of the colorful Hindu festivals Benefits of Ayurveda, Vastu, Vedic Astrology and gemology,
- Important insights of Dharmic life and how to begin.

The Dharmic path can provide you the means for attaining your own spiritual realizations and experiences. In this way it is as relevant today as it was thousands of years ago. This is the power of the Dharma since its universal teachings have something to offer anyone.

Published by iUniverse.com, 170 pages, 6" x 9" trim size, $16.95, ISBN: 0-595-39352-7.

Seeing Spiritual India
A Guide to Temples, Holy Sites, Festivals and Traditions

This book is for anyone who wants to know of the many holy sites that you can visit while traveling within India, how to reach them, and what is the history and significance of these most spiritual of sacred sites, temples, and festivals. It also provides a deeper understanding of the mysteries and spiritual traditions of India.

This book includes:

- Descriptions of the temples and their architecture, and what you will see at each place.
- Explanations of holy places of Hindus, Buddhists, Sikhs, Jains, Parsis, and Muslims.
- The spiritual benefits a person acquires by visiting them.
- Convenient itineraries to take to see the most of each area of India, which is divided into East, Central, South, North, West, the Far Northeast, and Nepal.
- Packing list suggestions and how to prepare for your trip, and problems to avoid.
- How to get the best experience you can from your visit to India.
- How the spiritual side of India can positively change you forever.

This book goes beyond the usual descriptions of the typical tourist attractions and opens up the spiritual venue waiting to be revealed for a far deeper experience on every level.

Published by iUniverse.com, 592 pages, $33.95, ISBN: 978-0-595-50291-2.

Crimes Against India:
And the Need to Protect its Ancient Vedic Traditions

1000 Years of Attacks Against Hinduism and What to Do about It

India has one of the oldest and most dynamic cultures of the world. Yet, many people do not know of the many attacks, wars, atrocities and sacrifices that Indian people have had to undergo to protect and preserve their country and spiritual tradition over the centuries. Many people also do not know of the many ways in which this profound heritage is being attacked and threatened today, and what we can do about it.

Therefore, some of the topics included are:

- How there is a war against Hinduism and its yoga culture.
- The weaknesses of India that allowed invaders to conquer her.
- Lessons from India's real history that should not be forgotten.
- The atrocities committed by the Muslim invaders, and how they tried to destroy Vedic culture and its many temples, and slaughtered thousands of Indian Hindus.
- How the British viciously exploited India and its people for its resources.
- How the cruelest of all Christian Inquisitions in Goa tortured and killed thousands of Hindus.
- Action plans for preserving and strengthening Vedic India.
- How all Hindus must stand up and be strong for Sanatana-dharma, and promote the cooperation and unity for a Global Vedic Community.

India is a most resilient country, and is presently becoming a great economic power in the world. It also has one of the oldest and dynamic cultures the world has ever known, but few people seem to understand the many trials and difficulties that the country has faced, or the present problems India is still forced to deal with in preserving the culture of the majority Hindus who live in the country. This is described in the real history of the country, which a decreasing number of people seem to recall.

Therefore, this book is to honor the efforts that have been shown by those in the past who fought and worked to protect India and its culture, and to help preserve India as the homeland of a living and dynamic Vedic tradition of Sanatana-dharma (the eternal path of duty and wisdom).

Available from iUniverse.com, 370 pages, $24.95, ISBN: 978-1-4401-1158-7.

The Eleventh Commandment
The Next Step in Social Spiritual Development

A New Code to Bring Humanity to a Higher Level of Spiritual Consciousness

Based on the Universal Spiritual Truths, or the deeper levels of spiritual understanding, it presents a new code in a completely nonsectarian way that anyone should be able and willing to follow. We all know of the basic ten commandments which deal mostly with moralistic principles, but here is the Eleventh Commandment that will surely supplant the previous ones and provide a truly spiritual dimension to everything we do. It increases our awareness of the spiritual nature all around and within us.

Herein is the next step for consideration, which can be used as a tool for guidance, and for setting a higher standard in our society today. This new commandment expects and directs us toward a change in our social awareness and spiritual consciousness. It is conceived, formulated, and now provided to assist humanity in reaching its true destiny, and to bring a new spiritual dimension into the basic fabric of our ordinary every day life. It is a key that unlocks the doors of perception, and opens up a whole new aspect of spiritual understanding for all of us to view. It is the commandment which precepts us to gain the knowledge of the hidden mysteries, which have for so long remained an enigma to the confused and misdirected men of this world. It holds the key which unlocks the answers to man's quest for peace and happiness, and the next step for spiritual growth on a dynamic and all-inclusive social level.

This 11th Commandment and the explanations provided show the means for curing social ills, reducing racial prejudices, and create more harmony between the races and cultures. It shows how to recognize the Divine within yourself and all beings around you. It shows how we can bring some of the spiritual atmosphere into this earthly existence, especially if we expect to reach the higher domain after death. It also explains how to:

- Identify our real Self and distinguish it from our false self.
- Open our hearts to one another and view others with greater appreciation.
- Utilize higher consciousness in everyday life.
- Find inner contentment and joy.
- Attain a higher spiritual awareness and perception.
- Manifest God's plan for the world.
- Be a reflection of God's love toward everyone.
- Attain the Great Realization of perceiving the Divine in all beings.

The world is in need of a new direction in its spiritual development, and this 11th Commandment is given as the next phase to manifest humanity's most elevated potentials.

This book is $13.95, Size: 6" x 9", Pages: 128, ISBN: 0-595-46741-5.

Yoga and Meditation
Their Real Purpose and How to
Get Started

Yoga is a nonsectarian spiritual science that has been practiced and developed over thousands of years. The benefits of yoga are numerous. On the mental level it strengthens concentration, determination, and builds a stronger character that can more easily sustain various tensions in our lives for peace of mind. The assortment of *asanas* or postures also provide stronger health and keeps various diseases in check. They improve physical strength, endurance and flexibility. These are some of the goals of yoga.

Its ultimate purpose is to raise our consciousness to directly perceive the spiritual dimension. Then we can have our own spiritual experiences. The point is that the more spiritual we become, the more we can perceive that which is spiritual. As we develop and grow in this way through yoga, the questions about spiritual life are no longer a mystery to solve, but become a reality to experience. It becomes a practical part of our lives. This book will show you how to do that. Some of the topics include:

- Benefits of yoga
- The real purpose of yoga
- The types of yoga, such as Hatha yoga, Karma yoga, Raja and Astanga yogas, Kundalini yoga, Bhakti yoga, Mudra yoga, Mantra yoga, and others.
- The Chakras and Koshas
- Asanas and postures, and the Surya Namaskar
- Pranayama and breathing techniques for inner changes
- Deep meditation and how to proceed
- The methods for using mantras
- Attaining spiritual enlightenment, and much more

This book is 6"x9" trim size, $17.95, 240 pages, 32 illustration, ISBN: 1451553269.

Avatars, Gods and Goddesses of Vedic Culture

The Characteristics, Powers and Positions of the Hindu Divinities

Understanding the assorted Divinities or gods and goddesses of the Vedic or Hindu pantheon is not so difficult as some people may think when it is presented simply and effectively. And that is what you will find in this book. This will open you to many of the possibilities and potentials of the Vedic tradition, and show how it has been able to cater to and fulfill the spiritual needs and development of so many people since time immemorial. Here you will find there is something for everyone.

This takes you into the heart of the deep, Vedic spiritual knowledge of how to perceive the Absolute Truth, the Supreme and the various powers and agents of the universal creation. This explains the characteristics and nature of the Vedic Divinities and their purposes, powers, and the ways they influence and affect the natural energies of the universe. It also shows how they can assist us and that blessings from them can help our own spiritual and material development and potentialities, depending on what we need.

Some of the Vedic Divinities that will be explained include Lord Krishna, Vishnu, Their main avatars and expansions, along with Brahma, Shiva, Ganesh, Murugan, Surya, Hanuman, as well as the goddesses of Sri Radha, Durga, Sarasvati, Lakshmi, and others. This also presents explanations of their names, attributes, dress, weapons, instruments, the meaning of the Shiva lingam, and some of the legends and stories that are connected with them. This will certainly give you a new insight into the expansive nature of the Vedic tradition.

This book is: $17.95 retail, 230 pages, 11 black & white photos, ISBN: 1453613765, EAN: 9781453613764.

The Soul
Understanding Our Real Identity
The Key to Spiritual Awakening

This book provides a summarization of the most essential spiritual knowledge that will give you the key to spiritual awakening. The descriptions will give you greater insights and a new look at who and what you really are as a spiritual being.

The idea that we are more than merely these material bodies is pervasive. It is established in every religion and spiritual path in this world. However, many religions only hint at the details of this knowledge, but if we look around we will find that practically the deepest and clearest descriptions of the soul and its characteristics are found in the ancient Vedic texts of India.

Herein you will find some of the most insightful spiritual knowledge and wisdom known to mankind. Some of the topics include:

- How you are more than your body
- The purpose of life
- Spiritual ignorance of the soul is the basis of illusion and suffering
- The path of spiritual realization
- How the soul is eternal
- The unbounded nature of the soul
- What is the Supersoul
- Attaining direct spiritual perception and experience of our real identity

This book will give you a deeper look into the ancient wisdom of India's Vedic, spiritual culture, and the means to recognize your real identity.

This book is 5 ½" x 8 1/2" trim size, 130 pages, $7.95, ISBN: 1453733833.

Prayers, Mantras and Gayatris
A Collection for Insights, Spiritual Growth, Protection, and Many Other Blessings

Mantra-yogaespecially for this ageUsing mantras or prayers can help us do many things, depending on our intention. First of all, it is an ancient method that has been used successfully to raise our consciousness, our attitude, aim of life, and outlook, and prepare ourselves for perceiving higher states of being.

The Sanskrit mantras within this volume offer such things as the knowledge and insights for spiritual progress, including higher perceptions and understandings of the Absolute or God, as well as the sound vibrations for awakening our higher awareness, invoking the positive energies to help us overcome obstacles and oppositions, or to assist in healing our minds and bodies from disease or negativity. They can provide the means for requesting protection on our spiritual path, or from enemies, ghosts, demons, or for receiving many other benefits. In this way, they offer a process for acquiring blessings of all kinds, both material and spiritual. There is something for every need.

Some of what you will find includes:

- The most highly recommended mantras for spiritual realization in this age.
- A variety of prayers and gayatris to Krishna, Vishnu and other avatars, Goddess Lakshmi for financial well-being, Shiva, Durga, Ganesh, Devi, Indra, Sarasvati, etc., and Surya the Sun-god, the planets, and for all the days of the week.
- Powerful prayers of spiritual insight in Shiva's Song, along with the Bhaja Govindam by Sri Adi Shankaracharya, the Purusha Sukta, Brahma-samhita, Isha Upanishad, Narayana Suktam, and Hanuman Chalisa.
- Prayers and mantras to Sri Chaitanya and Nityananda.
- Strong prayers for protection from Lord Narasimha. The protective shield from Lord Narayana.
- Lists of the 108 names of Lord Krishna, Radhika, Goddess Devi, Shiva, and Sri Rama.
- The Vishnu-Sahasranama or thousand names of Vishnu, Balarama, Gopala, Radharani, and additional lists of the sacred names of the Vedic Divinities;
- And many other prayers, mantras and stotras for an assortment of blessings and benefits.

This book is 6"x9" trim size, 760 pages, ISBN:1456545906, or 978-1456545901, $31.95.

www.Stephen-Knapp.com

Be sure to visit Stephen's web site. It provides lots of information on many spiritual aspects of Vedic and spiritual philosophy, and Indian culture for both beginners and the scholarly. You will find:

- All the descriptions and contents of Stephen's books, how to order them, and keep up with any new books or articles that he has written.
- Reviews and unsolicited letters from readers who have expressed their appreciation for his books, as well as his website.
- Free online booklets are also available for your use or distribution on meditation, why be a Hindu, how to start yoga, meditation, etc.
- Helpful prayers, mantras, gayatris, and devotional songs.
- Over a hundred enlightening articles that can help answer many questions about life, the process of spiritual development, the basics of the Vedic path, or how to broaden our spiritual awareness. Many of these are emailed among friends or posted on other web sites.
- Over 150 color photos taken by Stephen during his travels through India. There are also descriptions and 40 photos of the huge and amazing Kumbha Mela festival.
- Directories of many Krishna and Hindu temples around the world to help you locate one near you, where you can continue your experience along the Eastern path.
- Postings of the recent archeological discoveries that confirm the Vedic version of history.
- Photographic exhibit of the Vedic influence in the Taj Mahal, questioning whether it was built by Shah Jahan or a pre-existing Vedic building.
- A large list of links to additional websites to help you continue your exploration of Eastern philosophy, or provide more information and news about India, Hinduism, ancient Vedic culture, Vaishnavism, Hare Krishna sites, travel, visas, catalogs for books and paraphernalia, holy places, etc.
- A large resource for vegetarian recipes, information on its benefits, how to get started, ethnic stores, or non-meat ingredients and supplies.
- A large "Krishna Darshan Art Gallery" of photos and prints of Krishna and Vedic divinities. You can also find a large collection of previously unpublished photos of His Divine Grace A. C. Bhaktivedanta Swami.

This site is made as a practical resource for your use and is continually being updated and expanded with more articles, resources, and information. Be sure to check it out.